Confident Selling

CONFIDENT SELLING

James R. Fisher, Jr.

Parker Publishing Company, Inc.
West Nyack, New York

PRINTED IN THE UNITED STATES OF AMERICA
ISBN 0-13-167536-2
B & P

To my wife,
Pat

What This Book Can Do for You

This book is written for the man who has reached an impasse with himself. He may be confounded by a prospect, a peer, a boss, or even a wife. In any case, the result is the same—unnecessary worry and frustration, not to mention sluggishness and ultimately, inertia and no confidence in himself.

It is written for the man who is close, but still can't seem to "make it." That is to say, the hot prospect remains frustratingly just that—the hot prospect. Or the big break that he's been waiting for continues to allude him, even though he can feel it in his bones.

It is written for the man who finds himself making excuses to his family, friends, and employer for not closing the big sale or realizing the big promotion. Or the man who finds himself blaming everyone in sight—his boss, his wife, his kids, his colleagues, his customers, his prospects, even his minister, priest, or rabbi—everyone but himself for his failure to make satisfactory progress in his career, for his lack of confidence.

Indeed, it is written for the man afraid, a slave to worry, but who is not aware of it.

7

The author knows of this *fear*, this *frustration*, this *anxiety*—not out of books, but out of life. First as a chemist, then as a salesman, still later as a sales manager, and finally as a chemical company executive. Though the nature of his work was to change and he was to know more affluence and luxury, the battle remained always the same—a never ending contest with self. So intense did this battle become that he was to take the entire year of 1969 off to contemplate it. What he has learned from this self-imposed sabbatical, as well as from his past experiences, is the basis of this book.

This book is not a *how* book, nor a *what* book, nor a "Rah-Rah" book, but a *why* book: Why are we our own worst enemy; why do so many of us fail to find fulfillment in our work; why is 80% of the selling usually accomplished by 20% of the sales force; why do 10% lead while 90% follow; why do so many of us not have even the slightest notion of a purpose in life; why do we so seldom challenge our true potential; why do so many of us torture ourselves with doubts while giving others the selfsame benefit of the doubt? Yes, indeed, why, why, why?

It would seem to be a matter of fear—unmitigated, incomprehensible *fear*. This corrosive and destructive humor eats into a man making him ill-tempered, often forcing him to press or act in an uncharacteristic fashion—behavior, of course, which success will not condone.

Look around you. Do you think the fellow making all the sales has more talent than you? Is he really a better salesman? Why do you suppose the New York Jets' Joe Namath has such charisma? Certainly, there are other quarterbacks as good, if not better than him. What, then, makes him stand out? Peggy Fleming, queen of the figure skaters, thought him "a mess" until she met him. Then she was moved to say, "Gee, I think he's great . . . he seems to have so much fun." She could just as well have said, he is his own best friend. No matter what you think of this young man, I think you will agree that he is brutally honest with and about himself.

How about you? Do you accept yourself as you are? Do you have confidence in yourself? Or do you pretend to yourself, as you would pretend to others, to being someone else? Let us consider your boss, for instance. Do you think you are smarter, more capable than him? Why? Please, no glowing generalities! Could it be that you are captivated by the glamour and prestige of his position? Before one can seriously consider managing others, he must first have a firm hold on himself. Are you satisfied with your progress in this regard? Now ask yourself if you could really accept the long hours, the loneliness, the responsibility and sacrifice required of the job. The point being that whatever it is you think you want must blend well with what you need; whatever you think you are must mesh with what you really are. Wants sometimes confuse us on both counts. They can become a convenient way for us to hide the truth of ourselves from us. When this occurs, we start pressing. The joy of work is killed. And if something isn't done directly to correct this situation, our whole world can suddenly come apart. That is why we must step in and take charge of ourselves. In other words, it is in squaring ourselves *with ourselves* that we rediscover ourselves in our work, that we discover *confident selling.* For us to do otherwise only aggravates personal frustration, worry, and anxiety—throwing us further from our promise.

Fear is embedded in self-ignorance. Confidence in selling is grounded in knowing; in understanding why; in tolerating our inevitable ineptitude; in showing compassion,

9

not only for others but for ourselves as well; in giving us an insight into our particular dilemma and the tools for doing something about it.

This little book is designed to be a helper, a brain-tingler, in probing the depths of why. But it is not meant to be a substitute for self-initiative. So don't take comfort in the idea that you will read this and go back to being your normal sluggish self. It won't do and you know it. The gloves have been taken off because you want to see it and hear it like it is. Let's face it, you want answers and it turns out you're the only one who has access to them.

This book is purposely short so that you will be able to read it through quickly, perhaps in a single sitting. Then tuck it into your attaché case and forget about it; that is, *until you need it*. Hopefully, it will be a reminder to you that you are not alone on this journey. Don't let the confident masks we all like to wear in our clients' office lobbies fool you. Actually, we are all brothers under the skin—susceptible to the same doubts and misgivings as you.

But the monkey is on your back and only you can knock it off. Good luck to you in this venture from a guy who is still busy knocking monkeys for a loop.

James R. Fisher, Jr.

TABLE
OF CONTENTS

WHAT THIS BOOK CAN DO FOR YOU   7

CHAPTER 1—SELLING AND CONFIDENCE   21

Drive Forces of Salesmen • 22

—Acceptance
—Security
—Recognition
—Friendship
—Attention
—Ownership
—Status
—Association
—Responsibility
—Accomplishment
—Righteousness

13

CONTENTS

Three Parts of Every Good
Salesman • *24*

—Healthy Ego
—Fine Sensitivity
—High Energy Level

The Modern Salesman Is
Indispensable • *26*

Steps to Take the Worry and
Frustration Out of Selling • *28*

—Attitude
—Understanding
—Persuasion
—Motivation

Self-Study Questions • *29*

Recommended Further Reading • *29*

CHAPTER 2—SELLING AND YOU—THE
POWER OF A PROPER
ATTITUDE **31**

You Are in Command • *32*

You Are Needed • *33*

You Are Opportunity • *33*

14

The Best Person to Understand Is
Yourself • *34*

Hitting the Road to More Sales • *38*

How Attitudes Affect the
Salesman • *41*

How to Fight Worry from the
Beginning • *45*

The Importance of Controlling
Attitudes • *49*

Developing Controlled and
Enlightened Salesmanship • *55*

Ten Commandments of Selling • *57*

—Believe in Yourself Completely
—Believe in Your Company
Intensely, Emotionally,
Overwhelmingly
—See Yourself as a Successful
Salesman
—Expect to Make the Sale and
You Will
—Recognize the Importance of
Others
—Start Liking Yourself
—Desire to Create Something for
the Good of Others
—Look on Your Problems as
Door Openers to Increased
Opportunity

—Plan Your Work Well—Then
Work Your Plan
—Always Be Enthusiastic About
Everything That Embraces
Your Life

Self-Study Questions • 63

Recommended Further
Reading • 64

CHAPTER 3—SELLING AND OTHERS—THE
POWER OF EMPATHETIC
UNDERSTANDING   65

Four Keys for Understanding
Others • 66

—We All Love Ourselves
—We Are All Most Interested in
Ourselves
—Every Person Wants to Feel
Important
—Everyone Craves Approval from
Others

Look at the Prospect as a
Person • 69

Understanding the Three Levels of
Communication • 75

—Hearing Level

16

—Listening Level
—Thinking Level

A Checklist for Better Listening
Habits • 77

—Use Your Entire Body
—Give Mr. Prospect Your
Absolute and Undivided
Attention When He Talks
—Don't Impose Your Will on Him
—Don't Ever Argue
—Don't Make Him Feel Guilty
—Avoid Destructive Talk
—Don't Monopolize the
Presentation

Developing the Thinking Level of
Communication • 79

Self-Study Questions • 85

Recommended Further
Reading • 85

CHAPTER 4—OVERCOMING COMMON
OBSTACLES TO SUCCESS—
THE POWER OF SKILLFUL
PERSUASION 87

Four Keys to Human
Tendencies • 90

—We Tend to Resist Change
—We Tend to Prefer Thinking
Our Own Thoughts
—We Tend to Prefer Hearing
What We Want to Hear
—We Tend to Victimize Ourselves
with False or Unwarranted
Assumptions

A Checklist for Offsetting Invalid
Assumptions • 96

Techniques for Gaining Skill in
Persuasion • 103

—Encourage Cooperation
—Draw Out Your Prospect's
Thoughts
—Deal with the Prospect's
Emotions
—Listen to Your Prospect
—Give and Get Feedback of Your
Prospect's Thinking
—Hold Your Prospect's Attention
—Activate Prospect's Thinking
—Deal with Prospect Resistance

Meeting Resistance
Effectively • 121

How to Sell the Tough
Customers • 124

—Mr. Silent
—Mr. Procrastinator

CONTENTS

—Mr. Glad-Hander
—Mr. Methodical
—Mr. Overcautious
—Mr. Opinionated
—Mr. Skeptical
—Mr. Grouch
—Mr. Argumentative

Self-Study Questions • *136*

Recommended Further
Reading • *138*

CHAPTER 5—REASONS FOR SUCCEEDING
—THE POWER OF DYNAMIC
MOTIVATION **140**

What Is Motivation? • *144*

How to Understand
Motivation • *147*

How to Make Motivation Work for
You • *152*

How to Use Incentives • *158*

Self-Study Questions • *162*

Recommended Further
Reading • *163*

19

CHAPTER 6—THE FINISHING TOUCH FOR
CONFIDENT SELLING 166

Conquering Fear of Failure • 168

Salesmen Are Individuals • 172

Overcoming Fear with
Confidence • 175

Self-Study Questions • 177

Recommended Further
Reading • 178

INDEX 181

(1) Selling and Confidence

More and more salesmen are failing these days because they unconsciously conspire to place obstacles in the path of their success. Loaded with ability, product knowledge, technology, qualified prospects, and the promise of riches, they continue nevertheless to drop off or out of the selling race. This attrition is a very real cost to all concerned—the salesman, his company, and even the prospective consumer.

One statistic which has remained unchangeable is this: 80% of a firm's products or services are sold by 20% of its salesmen. Or conversely, 20% of the salesmen sell 80% of the firm's output in goods and/or services.

In other words, one good salesman carries in addition to his own load that of four poor salesmen. Perhaps this is not the case for members of your sales staff. If true, you are indeed fortunate. But let us suppose that your split is 70–30, or even 60–40. Is this satisfactory?

What, then, is the problem? The answer lies within each individual salesman. Some would call it the problem of motivation. Others would see it simply as a matter of training and management. Both are, of course, involved. Yet neither has proven totally successful to date because they involve forces beyond the reach of the man outside. Only the man *inside*, the salesman himself, can insure success. He must find within himself both the desire to do the job of selling required, and the resourcefulness to oppose possible interfering forces. The control of these interfering forces makes him a success despite himself.

What are these possible interfering forces? The complex of drive patterns which make the salesman go as an individual are:

- Acceptance
- Security
- Recognition
- Friendship
- Attention
- Ownership
- Status
- Association
- Responsibility
- Accomplishment
- Righteousness

As you know, these forces operate within all of us. Where a salesman becomes vulnerable, however, is in the degree to which he sometimes becomes committed or emotionally reliant upon them.

What happens when the salesman's emotional commitment is excessive? Aside from draining him of valuable

energy, it finds him shying away from his marketing responsibility, especially in areas of high sensitivity. Let us say that
he has an inordinate drive for friendship—an innocuous
enough drive on the surface. But should an important prospect show personal contempt for this particular salesman,
be it real or imagined, he is likely to see and feel himself
a failure. Moreover, chances are he will either react un-
characteristically towards this prospect, thus losing his trust
and business for sure, or he will invent an excuse (no doubt
a just reason in his own eyes) for not managing to visit this
prospect regularly. Neither the promise of riches nor the
threat of dismissal will save him from this sad course.

Does this apply to the veteran salesman as well? Perhaps. The veteran salesman may be actually more slave
than master to his own destiny. Though the accolades and
rewards of past effort and accomplishment lie behind him,
he knows that each day he is reborn in competition. The
fact that he is still selling, however, indicates that he has
mastered a good many of these drives. But closer scrutiny
of his sales record often reveals looming gaps in sales pene-
tration and/or development of his assigned marketing ge-
ography. Only too frequently, a fresh recruit brings in an
order from a priority prospect that the veteran salesman
insisted couldn't be touched. Such a cost in unrealized business is beyond computation. Then too, sentiment usually
favors the veteran, which he may be predisposed to use to
compensate for poor performance. Such a crutch, of course,
does him no good, as he is happy only when he is selling—
when he is competing and producing.

Specifically, then, what may cause this slowdown? The
conflict between what drives the salesman forward and
what holds him back. Demands—real or imagined—outside
himself, drive the salesman forward, while the protective

restraint of emotionally hard-won victories hold him back. That is to say, he may find himself calling on prospects who nourish him emotionally, passing by those that don't— no matter what their potential value may be. Once this pattern is established, it can, of course, snowball.

A salesman can suddenly prove a problem overnight should this conflict take hold of him. First, sales calls made go down; followed inevitably by a drop in sales production; and finally, absenteeism, usually in the form of psychosomatic illnesses, erases his value to himself and his employer. A mutual investment is now in serious jeopardy. At the same time, his decline may adversely affect the efficiency of other members of the sales staff. A common practice, which again at first glance appears harmless, is the practice of the troubled salesman cajoling his cohorts into taking long coffee breaks with him. In this way his worry, frustration, and anxiety becomes theirs. It is indeed a contagious humor.

Three Parts of Every Good Salesman

A good salesman is made of at least three essential parts: a healthy ego, a fine sensitivity, and a high energy level. When these interfering forces are in conflict—in the form of worry or frustration—these three parts (ego, sensitivity, and energy) may turn inward on the salesman, consuming his very life force. He can become only a shadow of the man he was or could become.

Fortunately, since worry is a state of mind before an event happens, it can be negotiated intelligently. How can this be accomplished? It can be done by developing an understanding of the cause-effect relationship of worry. This is the seat of the salesman's problem. Expose and treat it and the salesman can regain his former vigor, strengthened by the knowledge that he has successfully coped with himself. Then in the future he will recognize the danger signs, taking proper care to avoid such risks.

To expose worry for what it is (and is not) requires that the salesman get inside the *why* of his behavior and that of his prospects. No matter how fine his grasp of how to sell may be, this is not enough, unfortunately, when he has reached such an impasse with himself. Sales techniques and strategies fall short of giving the salesman an understanding of the interpersonal forces at work in the selling situation. His frustration often arises out of attempting to use these methods beyond their usefulness.

Quite commonly what a salesman is prone to do when he has reached a selling impasse is this: He uses a few variations of how to close (moving from overwhelming the no's, to penalty of delay, to minor-point assumptive, and back to summary close); this failing, he tries a gimmick or two, painting a somewhat incredulous picture of the special benefits to accrue; this also failing, he abandons all semblance of savoir faire, resorting instead simply to wearing the prospect down. At this point, operating totally in an atmosphere of luck, he either continues this fruitless course or admits a stalemate and moves on to greener pastures.

Once this pattern is established, unpleasant or challenging encounters become less and less tolerable. The salesman begins to read into situations meanings that aren't there. Consequently, repetitive calls become a reminder of his past failures. A problematic condition is taking hold of him. What happens to such a salesman?

His call frequency to emotionally taxing prospects gradually evaporates away until he calls on them seldom, if at all. But why is this? Does the salesman ever ask himself:

- *Why* won't Mr. Prospect buy from me?
- *Why* am I unable to stimulate his buying interest?
- *Why* do I seem to bring out the worst in him?
- *Why* do I continue to press?
- *Why* am I so upset when I have to call on him?

It is only too apparent that the question why seldom, if ever, enters the perplexed salesman's head. Many salesmen, in fact, are blocked from gaining an insight into their dilemma by real or imagined pressures or fears with which they tend to be shackled. For instance, they usually favor a quantitative rather than a qualitative approach to their selling problem. Activity is substituted for thinking through the situation. The number of sales calls made, not the number of sales, becomes their criteria. Consequently, when they most need to see things clearly, they can see hardly at all. I hope this little book helps to move them off this plateau.

The Modern Salesman Is Indispensable

Heretofore, selling and sales training have been conducted and coached in a well-defined groove. That they have been successful endeavors cannot be denied. Even so, they are proving less and less relevant to our present marketing needs. As technology reduces the edge of one manufacturer or supplier over another, the importance of manpower development looms ever larger, taking on a significance to match, if not exceed, the product or service being sold. In the final analysis, success or failure remains in the hands of a most imperfect entity—man. This electronic and

26

computer age we find ourselves in has not developed an adequate replacement for him. Far from vanishing, the modern salesman's flexibility and adaptability continue to make him an indispensable factor in the marketing equation. Good business dictates that his hidden fears be exposed and that his latent talents be cultivated. In spite of this fact, too frequently we find quite the opposite to be true. That is to say, the salesman's latent fears and misgivings can be seen surfacing while his real potential and efficacy remain buried—hidden to all, including himself.

For the salesman to realize his inherent potential, he must understand and accept himself as he is. What's more, he should favor his prospects with a similar perception and charity. His job function, or what is actually expected of him, should also be clearly in mind. And finally, he should be given the necessary freedom to grow. Should he be blessed with these conditions and insights, his intrinsic promise will evolve as naturally as the flower from its cultivated seed. Conversely, should he not have such a personal fix or be availed such an opportunity for growth, he will remain a pawn to his surfacing weaknesses.

It is for these pragmatic reasons that an in-depth understanding of the selling situation by the individual salesman is becoming increasingly imperative. But how do we go about this? Obviously, there are many possibilities. This is one.

Let us establish that a primary objective will be to take the worry and frustration out of selling for the salesman so that he may operate at maximum efficiency and capacity. A secondary objective, which is a near certain outgrowth of this, would be to realize a better understanding between the salesman and his management, thus making each more effective, if not more useful to the other.

There are four positive steps which might be taken to accomplish these objectives:

1. **Attitude:** The salesman should see himself first as an individual and then as a salesman.

2. **Understanding:** The salesman should explore how his personality affects, as well as effects, the prospect; he should probe the probable causes for prospect apathy, intransigence, hostility, etc.; he should widen his tolerance band by developing his empathy.

3. **Persuasion:** The salesman should consider in detail the common obstacles to success; he should explore why the art of communicating ideas is so difficult; he should attempt to discover areas of agreement upon which to build his selling ideas; he should cultivate his imagination.

4. **Motivation:** The salesman should try to discover what makes him run; he should attempt to separate his real and imagined aspirations, tracing their relationship to his success or failure; he should then use this intelligence to better understand prospect motivation.

A logical point of embarkation would seem to be with you.

SELF-STUDY QUESTIONS:

1. Imagine yourself completely confined to a hospital bed. Who would you choose to share your room if you could select any person whom had ever lived? Why?

2. Would you say that most men find more pleasure in their work or in their recreation? Please explain.

3. If you were financially secure and would not have to worry about money for the rest of your life, what would be your expressed goal in life?

4. Most people live to be existing rather than exist to be living. Please comment.

5. What would you say is more important: A man happy in work, but just getting by financially or a man miserable in work, but nevertheless making it big financially? Why? Do you think one can have the best of both worlds? How?

6. Select three drive patterns from the list provided in this discussion and explain what they mean to you.

7. Success is not an end, but a journey. What does this mean to you?

8. The most difficult decision to make is to decide what exactly it is you want to do. Please comment.

9. At this very moment, what would you really like to be doing? Why? Then, why are you doing this instead?

10. If you were given any three wishes you desired, what would they be—in the order of your preference? Why?

RECOMMENDED FURTHER READING:

David Abrahamsen, M.D. *The Road to Emotional Maturity* (Pocket Books, 1966).

David Dunn. *Try Giving Yourself Away* (The Updegraff Press, Ltd., 1947).

Erich Fromm. *Escape from Freedom* (Rinehart & Co., Inc., 1941).

Robert W. Henderson, Ph.D. *Helping Yourself with Applied Psychology* (Parker Publishing Co., Inc., 1967).

Richard H. Hoffman, M.D. and A. W. Pezet. *The Conquest of Tension* (Holt, Rinehart & Winston, 1961).

Basil King. *The Conquest of Fear* (Doubleday & Co., 1921).

Walter Lowen. *You and Your Job* (Greystone Press, 1958).

H. A. Overstreet. *The Mature Mind* (W. W. Norton & Co., Inc., 1949).

Wilhelm Reich, M.D. *Character Analysis* (Orgone Institute Press, 1949).

James K. Van Fleet, *Power with People* (Parker Publishing Co., Inc., 1970).

Samuel J. Warner, Ph.D. *Self-Realization and Self-Defeat* (Grove Press, Inc., 1967).

(2) Selling and You— The Power of a Proper Attitude

Welcome aboard! You are about to launch yourself on an adventure designed to take the worry and frustration out of selling. In many ways, your profession is both a vocation and an avocation. Consider the proportion of your life spent selling or thinking of selling. It doesn't leave much time for sleep, let alone pursuits of fun and pleasure, does it? Is this really fair to you or to your family? Of course it isn't.

Yet, your anxiety and concern over a prospect whom you can't seem to close remains a gnawing reality to you. Likewise, the account that seems to be in constant trouble, despite your efforts to the contrary, gives you little peace. Not only do these contingencies wreck your harmony, but they also succeed in keeping you constantly off-balance as well. Under the circumstances, you are a slave rather than the master of your own destiny. You might liken your predicament to that of a man precariously walking the plank, with no clear understanding of why.

Small wonder that many of you punish your minds and bodies living too fast, spinning your wheels in long hours of fruitless effort. You have come to accept worry as a necessary, if not logical part, of the selling equation. Well, it needn't be so. Step back off that plank! That's no place for the captain of his ship to be stationed. Quit punishing yourself! You are not the helpless victim, but the man in charge. Remember, worry is only a state of mind; you can tame this renegade spirit and become master and captain of your fate—not the fawning passenger you paint yourself to be.

Before we begin, however, if any doubts exist in your mind about selling as a profession, let us dispel them here and now. As a salesman:

1. **You Are in Command.** A wise man once said, "Nothing happens until someone sells something." Think about this. What other profession can make such a claim? There is no more important person in the economic machinery of this nation than you, the salesman. Nor is there a more powerful influence than that of the salesman, be the body social, political, cultural, or religious. You are the prime mover in this nation's development—without you there is only static. As a matter of fact, it is the "salesman" in the social critic, politician, cleric, or pedagogue that wins and sways the crowd to his point of view. At one and the same time, the salesman creates and meets human needs, increases employment opportunity, social well-being, and prosperity. Like a stone thrown on still waters, the ripple of the salesman's

activities affects this nation's very scale of living—from its inner reaches to its outer bounds.

2. **You Are Needed.** During the Great Depression of the 1930's, jobs were pitifully scarce. That is to say, if you are talking about nonselling jobs. Newspapers were glutted with opportunities for the would-be salesman in the 30's. Only the salesman could prime the pump of a debilitated economy. Only he could move the public-at-large off a cautious dead center. Only he could restore the confidence of enterprise in the free enterprise system which we so cherish. Today, your function as a salesman is even more prominent. You are better educated and more knowledgeable than your predecessor, not to mention more cosmopolitan. You are as at home in Bangkok as you are in Burbank. American business know-how is what the world wants and you can fulfill that need. It is your special talents that bring economy, safety, comfort, performance, satisfaction, and many other benefits to the users of your products and services.

3. **You Are Opportunity.** Someone has made note of the fact that several of our nations largest corporations were founded by men without the benefit of a college education. What they fail to mention is that —to the man—all of these men were consummate salesmen. They took an idea and ran it up to high stakes. But if it were not for their selling skills, they wouldn't have gotten it off the ground. Every one of these men believed in his idea and in himself as the instrument through which his idea would find life. Moreover, they all displayed the contagious enthusiasm, resilience, confidence, and drive that every salesman worth his salt possesses. Like you, they wanted to be a somebody. They saw to it that everybody who touched their lives was aware of their ob-

33

session. Whomever they were to meet, they would change. Nothing would remain as it had been. They would convince men to take chances who might otherwise never consider such daring—chances on them and their idea. Imagine yourself in this light. Have you ever taken note of how many customers and prospects use the words you have fed them to express "their" idea? Doubtlessly, you have captured their imagination and made them see themselves doing what you would have them do. They buy more than your wares; they buy you. Perhaps you have not knowingly tapped this inner resource to your full advantage. Chances are you have hardly explored this potential. But have no doubts, it is there for the tapping. If you want proof, look around you for evidence. Your influence is reflected in your friends, business associates, and acquaintances—everyone with whom you have had personal contact. As you obviously have meant opportunity for others, you must mine this same abundance for yourself. This will take the anxiety out of work and put new vigor in your step.

The Best Person to Understand Is Yourself

Before you can begin this journey profitably, it is most important that you have some understanding of yourself. If you are sensitive to the needs and desires of other people, consider yourself well-endowed and indeed fortunate. A salesman without sensitivity or awareness is no less handicapped than a blind and handless surgeon. But possessing these raw skills, the salesman can develop empathy and understanding. He can tune himself in to man and hear what he wants and needs. Yet, priceless as empathy and understanding happen to be, they remain useless tools unless in the hands of a professional salesman. This little book is designed to assist you in acquiring this skill. Let us now begin with you.

Perhaps, like many of us, you are convinced that once you know your product and service completely, you can sell anybody anything. Were this the case there would be no need, of course, for sales training. Selling would be simply knowing your product and letting the product sell itself. Your function would be like a catalogue or reference book, supplying the correct answers to technical questions on demand. Once Mr. Prospect had all the information, your job would be finished. This, to be sure, is not how it is at all.

Actually, you see Mr. Prospect in all his ignorance. Ponder this a moment. Whereas he could study your sales catalogue or literature in the privacy of his office or home without suffering embarrassment or the loss of face, your presence may very well make him combatant. The more he is aware that this is a contest, the greater is this possibility. On the other hand, were you not to initiate this call, it is less than likely that he would either read or seriously consider your proposal. Let this be a warning to the "literature peddlers" who would use this route as a substitute for selling, loading receptionists with bulletins and notes for Mr. Prospect. He may not want a confrontation, but all the attractive literature and ornate knowledge in the world will not budge him without it. A difficult prospect often shields himself from the salesman who has in the past unwittingly reminded him of his personal or professional deficiency. This is only compounded when this salesman allows specious knowledge and thinking to preempt his good sense and judgment while talking to Mr. Prospect over the lobby phone. In other words, a salesman, any salesman, would do well to refrain from "snowing" his prospect with technical platitudes and trade jargon. Neither the pretense of knowing, nor the actual possession of knowledge, then, is enough. Knowledge is a tool only insofar as it is applicable to conveying the necessary wisdom he requires to make a wise decision. It is a device employed to shed light on how you intend to ease his burdens. So it is well to remember, before you can be his problem solver, that you must first be his *educator*. He must be enlightened so that he will know and understand his need. Never minimize what you are asking him to do; namely, to give up what he knows and understands for something that he doesn't. This explains why human emotions run deep in every sales call. They cannot be ignored. As a matter of fact, how his emotions are handled determines to a great degree whether the salesman will succeed or fail with him. This is what selling is all about. You can start by first perceiving and then accepting his inevitable reluctance to change.

Change is an emotional experience which causes prospects to act quite illogically. Badgering them incessantly with logical presentations, without taking measure of their responsiveness, only infuriates and blinds them to your intended purpose. What's more, it causes you untold frustration and distress. It is then that you must ascertain the nature of your particular impasse. It is then that you should come to grips with yourself and reflect seriously upon your problem.

Have you ever wondered why certain new salesmen jump off to impressive records, knocking over account after account—business that you couldn't seem to touch? You study them in amazement. Perhaps they can hardly find their way back to the office, but yet, there it is—success

36

personified. Why? Did the thought ever occur to you that, at the moment, they're too ignorant to be afraid, too naive to be feared or doubted, too uninformed to be worried about price or competition or any limitations inherent in their goods or services, and too inexperienced to develop any stultifying bad habits? Time and time again it has been shown that the main obstacle to successful selling is the salesman, himself. Bad thinking and habits run together to haunt and crush many veteran salesmen into a shadow of their former selves. Should a salesman be too often rejected, too seldom accepted, he can fall prey to self-pity and self-indulgence. Soon he may be projecting the tired and losing image he feels himself to be. His journey is all downhill. Meanwhile, the neophyte goes merrily and successfully on his way. But then one day, much to his chagrin, he finds his bloom fading as new accounts become harder and harder to come by. Panic sets in. "Gonna buys" replace bona fide business. Suddenly, alibi-itis afflicts him—intensifying as first the big ones and then the small prospects slip through his fingers. Finally, he is reduced to complaining of being overworked and underpaid. The pressure builds. Joy has gone out of his work. Though he doesn't yet realize it, the exhaustion is largely mental and the pressure mainly self-imposed. If this were not enough, salt is soon poured on his wounded pride as a new tyro—a "hot shot" to him—comes on the scene, performing the same "miracles" which were once only his to know. Look back and reflect. Has this been the full circle of your experience? Or might you be approaching this disillusionment?

It is at such a time that a salesman is tempted to press or impress. In frustration and anxiety, he deepens his dilemma by worrying rather than working his way out of it.

Later we will cover how this rich bloom of the novice can be sustained by studying our successes and how we can circumvent the deadening inertia of worry.

Too little time is spent on why we succeed while we are succeeding, and far too much energy and time is devoted to why we fail when we are failing. Hall of Famer, Ted Williams, noticed early in his career that hitters in the throes of a slump would constantly change their batting stance and listen to everybody's advice. This, more often than not, threw off their timing and rhythm at the plate, prolonging rather than shortening their slump. Williams decided that wasn't for him. When he was hot, which was often, he would make a careful, even scientific, study of his success. Consequently, he seldom was involved in protracted periods of hitlessness. But when he was, he didn't abandon his stance. Instead, all the know-how of hitting that he could call to mind was carefully reviewed. Some little thing, like the white background of a stadium, would be discovered to be the fault. Once the "Splendid Splinter," as he was known, uncovered and then corrected for this, he was off on another hitting streak.

Hitting the Road to More Sales

Ted Williams took the chance out of hitting. He sustained a long career, interrupted by two service hitches in the military, without losing his touch. This defies the limits of natural ability. What it demonstrates is this: Raw talent, intelligently honed, can be an instrument of unbelievable continuous success—and might I add, happiness?

Selling is not unlike hitting. Every day we come to the plate. Many of us see this as a game of chance. In other words, we go to bat giving away two strikes. We come to believe in "selling streaks," measuring our good fortune as a combination of being at the right place at the right time with the right product or service. Others see it as little more than knocking on more doors than the other guy. Percentages mean nothing to the latter. Then, there are still others who, like Ted Williams, study their successes, making a science of their selling, while measuring their progress by keeping percentage figures of their sales calls to sales. When things are looking down, they know just what to do. There is no panic. They remain confident that the answer to their particular problem lies within their grasp, to be found somewhere in the knowledge of their previous successes. Regrettably, few of us bother to study ours. We choose instead to enjoy the fruits of our efforts, but to learn little from them. As a matter of fact, it is not until we have had a real dry spell that we stop to think about selling—and then it is in a negative climate. Speaking parenthetically, another irony that repeats itself with monotonous frequency is the fact that salesmen who need selling books least are the most avid readers—perhaps not so much to learn, but to explain their success to themselves as they would convey it to others. Then too, sales managers are known to study the art of selling much more determinedly after—not before—they have been made managers for somewhat the same reason. Let us hope that exploring the why of selling will, in effect, put the horse, rightfully, before the cart.

Consciously or unconsciously you have the tendency to transmit your fear, doubt, apathy, anxiety, or a myriad of other negative attitudes which you may harbor, because of a buried contempt for the prospect or a hidden displeasure with yourself. These have a way of making the sales call "no contest." That is, Mr. Prospect is quick to sense that your emotional vibrations do not favor him. Then, despite your efforts to the contrary, he will escape you. Since selling is successful only in a positive climate, this creates a wall between you and him. This wall, of course, must be razed before you can communicate with Mr. Prospect in a meaningful way—before you can begin to sell. Otherwise, you might just as well sell to a mirror, for he sees clearly that you have not his best interests at heart, but yours. On the other hand, a positive frame of mind finds this wall to be little more than an accessible hedge and the mirror only a window.

Now, none of us is always happy, enthusiastic, loving, charitable, or optimistic. We should, nevertheless, make every effort to be in this frame of mind, or close to it, when we prepare to make a sales call. Mr. Prospect is not interested in our problems, though he sometimes feigns interest, because he is dogged enough by his own. Your job as a problem solver is to give him relief, not more grief. You should lift him out of his doldrums by the sheer force of your ideas and your enthusiasm for improving his lot. To prepare yourself mentally for this undertaking, say to yourself:

1. I am happy, for I have my health and well-being.

2. I am confident, for I have valuable and useful know-how.

3. I am enthusiastic, for I have the best product and company behind me.

4. I am needed, for I am an able problem solver.

5. I am in command, for I have my prospect's best interests at heart.

6. I am a successful salesman, for I deserve my success.

At first it may seem silly, perhaps even a waste of time.

You, of course, will have to be the judge. Try it for one week and see if it doesn't buoy your spirits and put you in a positive frame of mind. Just as you can block out of your mind unhappy experiences, you can force yourself to think in the affirmative. Obviously, there must be sincerity on your part. To establish this foundation, understand that this is not a substitute for inner conviction. Mouthing the words while thinking negatively means certain failure. In fact, your attitude is the core to the whole thing. Believe that you cannot change and you will not change. Believe that this is a lot of nonsense and you will discover that this, indeed, is a waste of time.

How Attitudes Affect the Salesman

No single factor controls the salesman's destiny more absolutely than attitude. It can literally make or break him. We hear a lot about attitude, but what do we really mean? Attitude has been defined as the way in which we react without thinking to things, groups, situations, persons, or values. Attitudes are made more from the cement of early life experiences than from anything else. Most of our predilections can be traced to childhood events. The cement is soft and wet during the opening chapters of our existence and impressions are made easily. As we become older and these impressions turn to indelible marks in stone, it is quite difficult to erase them. They become nearly a permanent part of us. Should you desire to polish these attitudes in order to remove some of the rough edges, don't be surprised if a chisel and a sand blasting gun are necessary. We give up old attitudes reluctantly. New ones are formed in the same spirit. (Please refer back to the concept of change.)

This is not meant to discourage you before you have begun. But there is no point in making a difficult task seem easy when this is clearly not the case. Attitudes can be changed. However, real resolve is necessary to accomplish this aim. Anything less will surely fail.

No one is without attitudes. And not surprising, seldom, if ever, is there a unanimity of opinion. Consider these words. Now, write down your first thought. If you are honest with yourself, it should throw some light on your deep-seated attitudes or predispositions. The list:

1. Marriage
2. Books
3. Celebrities
4. Divorce
5. Money
6. God
7. Riots
8. Fear
9. Conservatives
10. Hell

Were you to have a friend or colleague play this game, chances are his responses would differ from yours. Mainly, because of our attitudes, words call to mind a panorama of intriguing mental picture images. It is in such pictures that we capture the color and texture of our behavioral style.

Stop and think a moment. Did it ever occur to you that people who disturb you do so because they fall into the pattern of one of your negative attitudes or predispositions?

Let's say that you are calling on a new prospect. Bald-headed, cigar in mouth, red-nosed, a jaundice pallor to his cheeks—this round little man with the soiled shirt and stained tie introduces himself as Mr. Prospect. Perhaps he reminds you of your beloved Uncle Charley. So with disarming charm you greet him warmly. Then again, imagine that your first impulse is not to greet him but to flee. You see him as another "dipso" and you wonder how you can extricate yourself from him without becoming his "boozing buddy." Perhaps you will see him in neither light. You might see him as simply a weak and vulnerable man—in other words, an easy sell. Without realizing it, you are guilty of prejudging him. And have no doubt, he will sense this from your opening mood. The whole rhythm and harmony of your approach has been thrown off-stride by not anticipating the effect his appearance would have upon you, leaving you—not the prospect—at a severe disadvantage. Several calls later, you are still wondering why he refuses to buy from you.

Does this sound farfetched? Then, read how one salesman lamented his woe on a sale lost:

We concluded our meeting with Mr. Prospect's staff. All the details were ironed out. Everything seemed in order. Nothing was left but his signature on the contract. He invited me into a small office adjoining the conference room to complete this detail. A peculiar and nauseous odor hit me in the face as I entered this room. In an offhanded manner, I mentioned to Mr. Prospect that whoever used this office must smoke the furniture, so pungent was this tobacco aroma to my nonsmoking sensitivity. Pen in hand, he looked up at me with a strange expression. Then, he smiled grimly and said that he wouldn't be able to complete this contract just now, using the excuse that he was already late for a meeting. Now, he even refuses to see me.

What so often makes the difference between success and failure in selling are the little things. Some would call this the application of *common sense*. Yet, is there anything more uncommon than common sense? In the foregoing, the expectant salesman let his guard down and did the unpardonable thing—he relaxed. It doesn't matter if this were but a moment. The fact remains that it killed the sale. A salesman saw his work completed and became comfortable, allowing a preconceived and somewhat unconscious "attitude" to slip from his flippant lips. It cost him dearly.

At the same time, there is no reason to fault yourself for having such attitudes. They are a part of you and more than likely will remain so. What you must do is recognize that they exist and that they may possibly get in your way. Analyze them for what effect they may have on your behavior. Then, endeavor to use them to your advantage. Accept the fact that you feel comfortable with some prospects and miserable with others. One of your professional requirements is to sell to all types, in all situations. This makes it imperative that you widen your tolerance band or attitude bridge. You can do this by getting inside your attitudes and exploring them for what they are and what they tell you about yourself. As you do this, you will find your understanding of other people growing. Where you recognize prospect sensitivities similar to yours, you should have the advantage of knowing what will please them as well as what will offend them. On the other hand, where the prospect's inclinations are the antithesis of yours, you will be aware of this and turn it to your advantage. Consequently, the very fact that you have strong attitudes, then, does not discount you from becoming an effective salesman. But it does demand that you understand the basis of your attitudes and control their effect upon your conduct or behavior.

Consider the alternative. You conclude that you can't sell big companies because, "they're all phoney, pencil-pushing, glad-handing robots, anyway." Your mind conjures up the picture of condescending, though incompetent, junior executives aimlessly and futilely racing about—in plush offices with the mirage of order—and you feel justified in your thinking. Your kind of prospect, on the other hand, is a man with his sleeves rolled up, tie loose and askew, with the grime of production on his arms. So you search for this certain type—this kind of guy that makes you feel comfortable—leaving countless valuable prospects unattended, uncultivated. Now this makes no sense at all, as I'm sure you will agree. Yet, this is exactly what many salesmen do. Refusing to take a careful look at themselves only finds them more seriously handicapped, cut off from their potential by the myopia of their emotions.

How to Fight Worry from the Beginning

This is when worry sets in, closely followed by the forces of despair—frustration and anxiety. Each time this salesman passes opportunity knowingly, he is hit with a pang of guilt. His failure to bring himself to call on these prospects makes him his own worst enemy. A little war goes on with each failure. Add to this the mounting pressure of making sales goals, not to mention supporting a family, and you have one very weary salesman.

But this need not be! Worry can be lifted from your shoulders. It involves no miracle, no instant formula, no catchy phrase. Only hard work and time are involved. Yet, this is like nothing compared to the effort and duration of worry. Have you come up with any ideas on how to reduce this mental drag of worry? Perhaps the following thoughts will fill in some of the voids in your thinking on this.

Understand that you don't have to assume to ever be anyone but yourself. The idea that you have to be an engineer to sell the engineer, or a college man to sell the college professor, or a man of sublime tastes and culture to sell the truly sophisticated man is disproven every day—not on television, in films, books, or magazines, but on the front line of selling. More time, energy, and money is wasted by salesmen insisting on trying to be all things to all men. If you take nothing else away from this book, take this idea: *be yourself.* On this alone, you will astound the world, to say nothing of yourself. Your good grooming, manner, understanding, and knowledge will come to life for Mr. Prospect. He will then be whatever you would have him be. Once you attempt to imitate or pose as you believe he would have you be, then the unique freshness of your appeal is poisoned. The atmosphere becomes rigged and you are the rigger. Unless you are a very good actor, this whole production will flop with a dull thud, props and all, destroying all hopes of a sale.

There is one rule of selling which cuts through all the elaborate cover and complexity with which it is wrapped:

> If you know your product, service, and program, supported by a sound rapport with yourself as well as others, you can sell anyone anything.

The key, of course, to the whole enigma of selling is you. Build a basic structure of integrity and strength of character around the true you and you will be on your way to success. Accept yourself and others will accept you. Believe in yourself and others will believe in you. Do this and when your mind attempts to con you into taking shortcuts,

always the long routes in the end, you will have none of it.
Mr. W. Shakespeare said it in these words:

> . . . to thine own self be true,
> And it must follow as the night the day,
> Thou canst not then be false to any man.

When you give the limitations as well as the assets of
your program, when you qualify your prospect and sell
him what he needs and can afford, when you are careful to
state that unless changes are made your product will not
perform economically, you show yourself to be an honest
man. And nothing profits a man more than being known
amongst friends and business associates as a person of character and integrity—a man, in other words, to be trusted.

Have you ever noticed that the people you trust also
trust you? It is no coincidence. This is one of the basic
mechanisms of interpersonal relationships. Then too, the
better you know yourself, the more understanding you are
of others; the more you love yourself, the more generous
you are towards others; the greater your exhilaration expressed in your work, the more magnetic you are found to
be. The force of your positive radiance affects every life in
your presence. Imagine what you mean to a prospect surrounded by problems and submerged in an atmosphere of
"office politics." You are like a breath of fresh air. He listens
to you, studies your quiet grace, feels your natural optimism,
and forgets. He is yours. You have moved him from this
time and place. Some would call this "romancing the prospect." Whatever you wish to call it, you can be certain
that his attention will be short lived and that you must
constantly bring him back to the subject at hand. This, of
course, is what selling is all about. For the moment, however, let the focus remain on you only.

Now, consider what effect you would have on this same

gentleman in a negative guise. Suppose you greet him like Mr. Sobersides, wishing to give the impression that you are a serious one, but he fails to be moved. Then you feign erudition, importance, and a practiced enthusiasm. Finding this unsuccessful, you shift your image to that of a meek and fawning supplicator—a poor soul just trying to get by. Perhaps in the course of this single interview you use your "whole bag of tricks." Meanwhile, Mr. Prospect sinks lower and lower in his chair. You have managed to compound, not lessen, his miseries. Have no doubt, he will take note of you—if for no other reason than to be too busy next time you call. You haven't taken him out of his environment. You have buried him in yours. You haven't shown him that you have his best interests at heart, but only your own.

Successful people are too busy working at success to worry about whether they appear successful or not. Perhaps this explains, better than any reason, why they are successful. On the other hand, some would still feel the need to give the impression of success at all cost. Many salesmen would seem to suffer from this success syndrome. Should it catalyze their efforts in that direction, then the guise of success has served them well. However, seldom does this appear to be the case. Running scared, they compound their dilemma by forcing the impression of being what they apparently believe themselves not to be—namely, successful. Salesmen who would do most of their selling at sales meetings or around the office—not on the front line where the score is kept—can be found playing this losing game. But I repeat, if they would only get inside their negative attitudes and give them the careful scrutiny they require, this could be avoided. Once you gain control of these disturbing attitudes, you cease being a slave to any man, least of all, yourself. But alas, not before!

The Importance of Controlling Attitudes

Let us examine precisely why attitudes are so important to us and in doing so find why they are so difficult to change:

1. Attitudes appear to heighten certain aspects of our environment. We may love homelife, but abhor the hustle and bustle of city life—or quite the converse of this.

2. Attitudes seem to give us simplified definitions of life situations. Therefore, some would see Jews as having all the money and Blacks as having none; the Republican Party as being the party of big business and the Democratic Party as being the party of the little man.

3. Once you have adopted an *attitude*, there is a tendency to rationalize in a manner to justify having it. You read the annual report of your bank and note that one of the members of the Board of Directors is Jewish. So you say, "See here . . . those Jews have got all the money"—meaning, of course, this is surely proof enough.

Perhaps the best way of seeing attitudes is to realize that they make us more comfortable being the way we are as people. Earlier, mention was made of the salesman trying to be all things to all people. The temptation to do this is most apparent when we are least comfortable or under the greatest (real or assumed) stress. When we are most comfortable, our whole personality from the ugly to the beautiful inevitably unfolds. Usually, we allow our personality to unfold only in the privacy of our home. Pretending stops at the front door because we know that love and security lie within—a sanctuary from the menacing world outside. We feel no need to perform falsely. We are accepted for what we are and for what we are not. Many times this results in a striking change in our personality. Accompanying a salesman on his calls and then home after the day's work has been completed is a graphic case in point. Most frequently you find yourself in the company of two totally different people. It has been my experience that where the change is less striking, the salesman is happier and more successful in his work. Furthermore, it is no small coincidence that where you find a devoted and understanding wife, not to mention respectful and loving children, the salesman has a firm and healthy image of who he is.

Incidentally, the problems a salesman encounters on the job can become quite baffling to his wife because of his quasi-schizophrenia. I'm sure you have been told many times that you are a great guy when you are yourself. Well, your wife builds her confidence, faith, and yes, hope, on just that—the best you. She can picture you as nothing less than successful because she sees you strong and true at home. Small wonder that she becomes angered and perplexed when you "strike out" on the job. Though you may see this as a lack of sympathy for your situation, it is hardly that. She knows what you are made of, perhaps far better than you. As a matter of fact, if you are able to bring yourself to discuss some aspects of your job "hang-up" with her, I'm sure you will find her an excellent sounding board. This applies especially to the area of attitudes.

No attempt will be made to suggest that you can see yourself as you really are. This is truly an elusive pursuit for us all. Fortunately, we can glean some invaluable light in understanding the natural deception we are prone to display as human beings. Each of us attempts to accomplish the satisfactions of life and to win the approval of others in a variety of ways. This is an important spark in our life force. Consider these interesting possibilities:

1. **We Rationalize.** To justify an action, we may say, "I did it because it was my understanding that you expected me to do it"; or, "I did it because if I hadn't we would have lost the business"; or, "I did it, frankly, because I saw no other way out . . ." In each case a good reason is provided for our behavior or action, which at least justifies it in our own minds.

2. **We Project.** If a fault doesn't suit us at all well, we may see it as the other fellow's problem. So we say, "Now you know Fred is careless and irresponsible. More than likely they quit us because of the way he handled their account while I was on vacation . . ."

3. **We Compensate for It.** This is illustrated when we put most of our time and energy into interests in which we are strong while disregarding or neglecting areas of weakness. To wit, you may say, "No, I don't agree that I need more sales training. After all, I've been selling for ten years. I'm a good salesman. Don't I make all my scheduled calls? Do you ever have to wait for my paper work? No one reads company literature any more conscientiously than I do. Can I help it if I'm in a poor selling territory? I'm going as hard as I can go!" As you can see from this example, "busy work" is used to compensate for the real work of selling. Compensation has been used as an excuse for not tackling a perplexing selling problem. Nonproductive salesmen are notorious for using this out. A less obvious way you may compensate is the route of making the work load of a co-worker your main concern. For instance, instead of working out your sales problems, you tackle his with reckless abandon. Suppose a new salesman comes into your territory. Though your manager has assigned him a training

program and a trainer, you make it your business to take on this responsibility. Meanwhile, your personal preparation for sales calls becomes something approaching tokenism—justified, no doubt, in your mind, by the fact that you are "helping" someone else. Does that sound familiar?

All of us use these various mechanisms at one time or another. They are indeed necessary in order for us to tolerate or even live with ourselves. But they can, and sometimes do, get in the way of our progress if not our emotional well-being. It is for this reason imperative that we understand these particular mechanisms—what they are and how they work. This knowledge can prevent them from dictating our behavior. A salesman can ill afford to react to a situation without thinking, without reflecting. There is no room for vanity. What he must do is reflect and understand why he has found the conduct of others disturbing to him. Or why he never seems to find time to call on certain prospects. Much as the salesman may dislike criticism, it would be well for him to make note of the fact that he is probably his severest critic. The distress and anxiety which can build up within him, especially during periods of poor selling, is an anathema to his professional and personal progress. It tires him emotionally and drains him physically. At precisely such moments, he can become dependent upon these mechanisms for reassurance and support. Since this is nothing more than negative support, the salesman is thrown further off course. His security threatened, worry is substituted for constructive action.

An honest appraisal of your many attitudes should be on your agenda. Think about what it is that makes you comfortable and content. What can rock this tranquility? As you think of this, remember that attitudes relate to the way we react to things, groups, situations, persons, or values. Success and happiness can be found as a salesman only when we recognize ourselves without the veneer.

Possibly you have overheard others talking about you, unknown to them. Did it make you angry? Well, it shouldn't. What you actually heard was simply the way the outside world sees you. Perhaps you were surprised to find their impression of you contrary to the one you were certain you projected. People see us more clearly than we would suspect. Prejudice and pettiness aside, they accept us as we are far better and more willingly than we accept ourselves.

To put this matter of attitude into clear focus, allow me to introduce you to Tom, a promising new salesman with a problem:

Tom was very jealous of his technical knowledge. He had an impressive background and had achieved a good academic record at the University. In fact, he displayed all the attributes of a born winner—attributes which should have certainly assured him success as a technical salesman. Yet, in truth, he was failing miserably. Several large accounts started to become vulnerable shortly after he had been assigned their service. Finally, his District Manager felt that something had to be done. He arranged a meeting with Tom to discuss his puzzling difficulty. Tom carefully prepared himself in advance of this meeting, developing what amounted to a prima facie case of justification for his conduct. It was obvious, from his point of view, that his customers were at fault. As Tom concluded his remarks, the seat of his problem was clear to his manager. Each time Tom would be posed a hard technical question outside his current range of comprehension, he would become argumentative. What's more, he was cleverly using his limited knowledge to "win" these arguments with technical "snow jobs" while remaining undaunted by the possibility of losing his prospects' business. Further probing revealed that he found it necessary to be condescending as well as overwhelming in order to protect his fragile ego. When his manager made him aware of the source of his problem, Tom was shocked. It had never occurred to him that he might be at fault. With the problem in the open, Tom and his manager were able to negotiate the delicate ground between *reaction* and *reflection*. A tentative plan was developed, designed to correct this faux pas. Each call thereafter, Tom was reminded to tell himself whenever he saw red: "Sell don't tell; reflect don't react!" In addition, he was cautioned to inform his prospects in an understandable way what his basic function was: to wit, that he was a salesman trained to give them the results they needed; that scientific or technical questions beyond his comprehension should be referred, through him, to the proper technical authorities in his company; that this was part of his service to them. Gradually Tom came to appreciate that prospects and customers were not out to get him, or to make him look bad. Their curiosity came to be understood as a measure of their interest. Referring such questions to the scientists and technical specialists made him more cognizant of the team effort involved in selling. Moreover, it widened his band of technical comprehension. Soon technology was proving to be an invaluable sales tool and not an end in itself. Not surprising, the road at first was rocky if only for Tom's self-imposed obstacles. But once he'd fought his way through this initial difficulty, he knew better than ever who he was and what his role was in the selling situation. It wasn't long until his change in attitude was gaining him the acceptance and respect

he so badly needed, not to mention its contribu-
tion to his steady growth as a salesman.

Developing Controlled
and Enlightened Salesmanship

Doubtlessly, you are a salesman because of a liking for
people and a sensitivity for understanding their needs. More
than likely, you are also egocentric and driven by a high
energy level. You may be a tremendous extrovert or a low-
key, withdrawing introvert—the point being, of course, that
it doesn't really matter. There is no single type of salesman.
Sensitivity, ego, and energy level may be your only common bond. Consider this combination. Pretty explosive,
wouldn't you say? How you handle this power pack, then,
holds the key to your development as a salesman. Controlled and used with enlightened practice, it becomes an
instrument of unimaginable force and possibility. Uncontrolled and used in a capricious manner, it might very well
consume you, burning you out long before your time. Unfortunately, there is no middle ground for the salesman.
Either he succeeds or fails; either he gets the order or he
doesn't. Success, health, happiness, and wealth come only
to those who understand this.

Some would call themselves salesmen while burning
up precious energy explaining away their failure to make a
scheduled appointment, or to get that order, or to find the
time for sales planning. While these would-be salesmen
are explaining away their dilemma, the *salesman* is knocking on doors. Selling to him is more than a challenge. It is
a way of life. Each sale is more than a conquest. It is a
reminder that he is needed. This awareness gives him the
grit to accept rejection philosophically. In each "no" he

sees opportunity—a new chance to educate. Meanwhile, his counterpart slowly atrophies as he nurses one psychosomatic ailment after another. In refusing to go the extra mile—to make that extra call—he deludes himself with the idea that he is a salesman, fortified no doubt by countless coffee breaks and cocktail hours. He is content shooting the breeze while the salesman is having all the fun, closing the accounts that are always waiting to be closed.

There is a lot of driftwood in every sales force. That is why 80% of a firm's products or services are generally sold by 20% of its salesmen. What is most appalling about this ratio is the fact that most salesmen want to sell and are capable of selling. Their problem lies between their internal conflict and external confrontation. This is well reflected in these sorrowful statistics:

> 42.2% of salesmen in a 1,000 retail merchant's survey made one call and quit; 24% made two calls and quit; 14.7% made three calls and quit; 12.7% made four calls and quit.

That meant that only one salesman out of eight made as many as four calls on a new prospect. Think of this. Only one salesman had the guts, conviction, and tenacity to keep plugging after seven of his "professional" colleagues had dropped out of the contest. What happened to these other seven guys? Would you happen to be included in these statistics? Where, would you imagine? Let us hope that you would see yourself as the persistent one. On the other hand, "where," or "when," or "what," or "who" are not our concern here, but "why" is. And "why" involves many personal factors, not the least of which is attitude.

James Allen once declared that a man is literally what he thinks. That is to say, it is not enough to know. There are no rewards for the salesman who knows prospect psychology, the anatomy of the sales call, the dramatic appeal of visual demonstrations, the fine and gentle art of persuasion, and learning of a similar ilk if he does nothing with it. If knowledge is used as an excuse or a screen for thinking, it is excess baggage to the salesman. Likewise, thinking used only as a game of mental gymnastics remains a poor tool in the hands of a salesman—a poor tool indeed. Some salesmen would turn to a book, such as this, to soothe their waning psyches. In other words, this would replace action. For those of such inclinations, they need read no further. This is not for them. Never mind impressing your cohorts with your professional wisdom or comforting yourself with the security found in "new" ideas. You will be terribly disappointed. First of all, what you are reading here is not new. And secondly, it is written to save you from your many crutches—not to provide you with another.

In order to take the worry out of selling, you must start with complete personal honesty with yourself—no games. Otherwise, there is no point in making the attempt. Anything less will find the book failing you and you further failing yourself.

Ten Commandments of Selling

A positive mental attitude is an absolute must. A periodic review of these ten commandments of selling should assist you in realizing this:

1. **Believe in Yourself Completely.** Have faith in your ability to do anything you desire.

2. **Believe in Your Company Intensely, Emotionally, Overwhelmingly.** Believe your company has the best products, people, and services. Believe you possess the best programs and products available to give the

results your customers want and need. Believe you
are a problem solver of the first rank, trained to do
a complete and professional job for each client.
Have faith in yourself, knowing that you have the
the ultimate in technical and moral support from
your company. Know that each success starts with
the decision to believe.

3. **See Yourself as a Successful Salesman.** Develop a
self-image of success; allow your mind to capture the
vision of the success you desire and it shall be yours.
See yourself as the leading salesman in your geog-
raphy and division. Keep success in the forefront of
your mind and it shall be yours. But be as patient
with yourself as you are with others. Realize that
success comes to those who have the courage to wish
and the patience to wait. If this would seem somewhat paradoxical, don't be dissuaded—it is! You
must be impatient with yourself to grow. At the
same time, you must be reasonable with others and
other things, be they obstacles, failures, or simply
provokers. Success comes to those who would per-
severe rather than provoke or procrastinate. Success
comes to those who make the "hopeless calls," tolerate and then defend late delivery of promised orders, or never know when to quit.

4. **Expect to Make the Sale and You Will.** Believe
you will find Mr. Prospect in a buying mood; expect to be well received, and you will be. Fight the
temptation of making calls a numbers game. The
total number of sales contacts has merit, but it is
no substitute for rolling up sales. Don't fall prey to
this numbers game; demonstrate in appearance,
voice, and spirit that you expect to close on every
sales call.

5. **Recognize the Importance of Others.** Become

other-people oriented; be humble without being obsequious. Search for ways of increasing your power of empathy. Remember people accept us pretty much as we accept them. Show kindness, thoughtfulness, consideration, and it will be reciprocated. Don't be deterred by a hard exterior. Prospects who use this guise are often protecting a very sensitive and vulnerable interior. Once they are won, they become your most devoted boosters.

6. **Start Liking Yourself.** Earlier in this discussion it was mentioned that the more you love yourself the more generous you are towards others. This is only too true. There is no doubt that the hardest person to make friends with is ourself. Love yourself and you will have no stomach or time for malevolence. Self-doubt will melt away. At peace with yourself, you will make your peace with everyone you meet. They will feel the soothing warmth of your calm. Make no mistake, the person of deep bias and poisonous hate is more at war with himself than those with whom he would hate. A salesman has no room for such negative forces. Think charity, have faith, maintain hope, and you will know love.

7. **Desire to Create Something for the Good of Others.** See in your work a vital connection with the fabric of life; desire to enhance the quality of this fabric; desire to refine your personality, to improve your mind and body, to accumulate wisdom and knowledge, to help your family, to succeed in business, to make money, to increase your gifts and talents, and to elevate your standard of life and that of those within the sphere of your influence.

8. **Look on Your Problems as Door Openers to Increased Opportunity.** As a problem solver, you will grow in a sense of worth and value to those whom

you would serve. Find confidence in your skill and the knowledge that you are needed. Understand that your professional stature is enhanced by difficulty, not by an unconstrained routine. What need would there be for a doctor without illness? Or a dentist without crooked teeth or caries? In the same breath, then, what need would there be for salesmen if products, services, or programs could be promulgated without personal cultivation and education, or would work without a hitch?

9. **Plan Your Work Well—Then Work Your Plan.** Where do you want to go in life? A plan suggests a purpose. What is your basic purpose of living for the future? Set goals on a daily, weekly, monthly, and yearly basis. Measure and evaluate your progress against your own set of standards. Don't leave this to someone else. Be your own man by proving that you are your own man. This is your ride through life. Are you riding in the pilot's chair or are you occupying the passenger's seat? This does not mean that you must be a captain of industry to count. On the contrary, it means only that you should be no less than captain of your destiny.

10. **Always Be Enthusiastic About Everything That Embraces Your Life.** There is no more contagious humor than that of genuine enthusiasm. It brightens the spirits of a depressed man more quickly than any tonic. And it makes for a new day for someone in the doldrums. Sheer enthusiasm can make a success of a poor plan; whereas, a lack of it seldom makes a good plan work. Negative forces turn tail when enthusiasm is about. It is the most vital aspect of the successful salesman. Without it, a salesman appears vitiated.

Repeat these rules often. Use them as reminders to you to think confidently as well as positively. Whatever you wish to achieve is attainable. Your mind is loaded with valuable tools to see that you do. Don't allow them to collect rust. Pick them up and use them. Some of these tools for your information are:

>imagination   vision
>reason   logic

They are all in your tool shed—found no less abundantly than in your colleagues' House of Intellect. Obviously, in your journey to this point you have had occasion to use them. But has there been any strategy, any system to their employment? If not, are your dreams to remain just dreams? Take courage in this old saying:

>What man can conceive,
>He may achieve.

See yourself successful and you will be successful. Imagine where you wish to be five years from now and you will arrive—on time. It is all up to you.

This chapter has asked you to become somewhat introspective. There is no other way to reach the inner you. There is no other way of knowing oneself. This is a relevant consideration, moreover, because a salesman's success is closely allied to his acceptance in interpersonal relationships. It is hoped that by knowing yourself better, you will become a more confident person. As your interior world, the world within, becomes an environment of beauty, order, and harmony, the world without will take on a similar shape and hue. This is our hope. Goethe spoke of this interrelation between the mind and destiny in these words:

Sow a thought, reap a habit.
Sow a habit, reap a character.
Sow a character, reap a destiny.

And finally, Bryan said, "Destiny is not a matter of chance. It is a matter of choice. It is not something to be waited for; but, rather, something to be achieved." Most of us feel more assured when we are driving an automobile, rather than being driven by someone else. Worry and anxiety crop up when we are pretending to be driving, while we are in fact actually being driven. Therefore, let us begin by giving you the wheel.

SELF-STUDY QUESTIONS:

1. Write a half-page sketch of the person whose character you admire most; you admire least.
2. Write down ten things, in the order of your preference, that you most want out of life.
3. Describe your job in one sentence.
4. Describe a selling experience that gave you a "lift." Describe one that depressed you.
5. Write down the following facts:
   a. What is my basic purpose in living for the future?
   b. What do I most want out of life?
   c. Is my goal money or personal achievement? Is it both, or something else? What?
   d. Analyze your past mistakes in life and ask yourself these questions:
   What mistakes did I make?
   What should I avoid in the future?
   Do I have sufficient desire to achieve success?
   Do I let myself be influenced negatively by others?
6. Sit down each day for at least 15 minutes and review the day's activities. What would you do differently? What would you have avoided? What could you have done to improve yourself or your situation in life this day?
7. Analyze your surroundings and ask yourself:
   Do I have order in my environment?
   Is there harmony between myself and my colleagues, between myself and my family?
   What can I do to improve my personal surroundings?
   Do I try to create harmony and beauty at home, at work, and at play?

RECOMMENDED FURTHER READING:

Claude M. Bristol. *The Magic of Believing* (Prentice-Hall, Inc., 1957).

Claude M. Bristol and Harold Sherman. *TNT: The Power Within You* (Prentice-Hall, Inc., 1954).

Bob Conklin. *The Dynamics of Successful Attitudes* (Prentice-Hall, Inc., 1963).

Napoleon Hill and W. Clement Stone. *Success Through a Positive Mental Attitude* (Prentice-Hall, Inc., 1960).

Louise Snyder Johnson, Ph.D. *Inside Your Mind* (Parker Publishing Company, Inc., 1965).

Rhoda Lachar. *You Are Unlimited!* (Wilcox and Follett Co., 1952).

David J. Schwartz, Ph.D. *The Magic of Thinking Big* (Prentice-Hall, Inc., 1959).

Alfred Uhler. *Discover Your Real Assets* (The Citadel Press, 1962).

Auren Uris. *Mastery of People* (Prentice-Hall, Inc., 1964).

(3) Selling and Others— The Power of Empathetic Understanding

Wouldn't it be a pleasant task in selling if we could read our prospect's mind? Just imagine how easy it would be if human beings thought and behaved like the characters we find in television dramas, the newspaper funnies, novels, films, or plays. We could get quick readings on them all with little, if any, difficulty. But, of course, this is not the case. People hardly ever behave as we would have them.

Notwithstanding this, there remains the same temptation for the salesman, as there seemingly is for everyone, to pigeonhole or categorize all people. In the flush of sales combat, a salesman may be tempted to see fat men as jolly and easy to sway; dark-complexioned men with swarthy skins and sharp noses as cunning, unscrupulous, and not to be trusted; men with red hair and fair skin as temperamental; those with receding chins as wish-washy; men with high foreheads, deeply socketed eyes, and broad brows as intellectuals; and those with big flopping ears as fools. Obviously, yielding to such temptation invites nearly certain embarrassment, if not disaster. There is no room for understanding in such frivolous prejudgments. On the contrary, character and personality analyses of this prefunctory quality tend only to carry the salesman further from, rather than closer to, a "meeting of the minds" with Mr. Prospect.

Since a salesman's primary job involves getting through to people, he must know and understand others as individuals—not as conveniently collective stereotypes. A salesman cannot risk a categorical approach under any circumstances and expect to be effective. Fortunately, most good salesmen appear to have a well-developed "seventh sense," intuition if you prefer, which prevents them from making fools of themselves. This sense enables them to remain flexible and keenly aware of any changing nuances in the sales situation. Such an endowed salesman allows the prospect to project his preferred self-image before he makes his move. A common expression used to cover this nebulous stratagem is, "I'll play it by ear." This simply means that the salesman does not intend to show his hand or commit himself to a course of action until he has had a chance to study and evaluate the prospect, no doubt taking careful measure of his mood and disposition of the moment.

Four Keys for Understanding Others

An inexperienced salesman cannot be expected to act with the same aplomb and deftness as the veteran salesman, any more than he can be expected to comprehend the implicit and explicit message of this text in a single reading. This is a supplement, not a substitute, for experience. It is in selling that the hard realities have a way of coming to life. However, you can be shown some signposts which may speed up your progress and your process of growth. Remember these signposts. They are the four cornerstones of the foundation for understanding other people:

1. We all love ourselves. Therefore, we are all egotists.
2. We all are more interested in ourselves than in anyone else in the world.
3. Every person you meet wants to feel important. He wants you to see him as special, for everyone wants to amount to something.
4. There is a craving in us all for the approval of others, so that we may in turn approve of ourselves.

Once the prospect senses that you, the salesman, have his best interests at heart and not your own; once he realizes what's in it for him; and once he reaches a clear understanding with you—the impossible becomes a matter of routine. But the road to that end is not without difficulty. And perhaps at the very center of this difficulty is this polarity: you must not only constantly cope with yourself, but with your environment as well. Other people, of course, fall into the latter grouping. People, then, may constitute part of our "menacing" environment. To illustrate: whereas you must feed Mr. Prospect's ego, he may step on yours; whereas you must generate and sustain interest in his plight, he may demonstrate no such inclination towards yours; whereas you must contribute to his sense of self-esteem, he may denigrate yours; and whereas you must accept and approve of him without qualification, he may deny you a similar courtesy. Being intelligent and sensitive, this is often found to be a frustrating, if not a totally impossible, row to hoe. Many salesmen are torn between self-love and self-abnegation. They go through the motions of selling, but fail to put their heart into it. Inside they are broken men. That is precisely why a near clinical understanding of others, not to mention oneself, is so fundamental to our goal of taking the worry out of selling. Without a perspective on the interpersonal forces at work in the sales situation, the salesman is at the mercy of his uncontrolled inherent nature. Nothing could be less reassuring.

Let us now probe into this world of ideas and behavioral patterns in the hope of knowing and understanding others, to the benefit of both participants. Along the way, you should be able to visualize what makes for easy rapport and why; what is necessary to cultivate different types of people and why; and what creates an atmosphere of genuine empathy. Any progress you may make in this direction should favor you with a more pleasant climate to sell in the sales interview.

Not so long ago, an American doctor wrote an amusing and informative book called, *The Games People Play*. It was Dr. Berne's contention in this work that each of us hungers for some sort of emotional recognition, without which our inner person's ego would shrivel. In Dr. Berne's lingo, each action that satisfies this hunger is called a "stroke." He claims that whereas a film actor may require a hundred strokes to his ego per day, a scientist may be content with one a year from a respected colleague. Incidentally, this would explain why stars of the stature of Frank Sinatra and Sammy Davis, Jr. are surrounded by sycophants. Moreover, it would render obvious why Dr.

Berne makes frequent references to salesmen, showing how they utilize this psychology in their daily selling. This, of course, can be a dangerous device in the hands of a salesman who is unaware of the weapon he wields. Like a knife, it can shape a thing of beauty or gore a thing to death. Knowing this, to be sure, makes for a more precise handling of this delicate instrument—emotion.

Thus, an awareness of the differing emotional needs of our prospects is the first step towards successful selling for the professional salesman. If it were otherwise, we would be bringing down our prospects with a shotgun instead of a rifle. We would be approaching the scientist as we would approach the insecure artist. In other words, we would be making selling a game of luck and not a profession of skill. Note that the essence of our function in the overall marketing scheme is that we have a peculiar ability to call on all types in all situations and to sell to them as individuals. "Fine," you say, "but how does one go about developing this ability?"

Look at the Prospect as a Person

Our prospects provide us with openers. Take the lid off a man and you discover that he has a pretty fixed self-image of himself. But fail to recognize this fact and you will find yourself in immediate trouble. For instance, have you ever made what you considered an innocent comment only to have the prospect react vehemently? Well, if you have, it is more than likely that you have unwittingly bumped head-on into his fragile self-image. What sometimes makes this even more perplexing is that another person might say the same thing without triggering a reaction. You scratch your head in literal bewilderment. "Why?"

keeps pounding at your brain. The answer lies probably well-concealed in Mr. Prospect's self-image. We can only wager a guess as to what this might be. Two rather fundamental premises, however, may assist us in making this surmise with good judgment:

1. Consider how he sees you.
2. Consider how he thinks you see him.

It is surely no accident that salesmen in the main are moderate, if not conservative, in their attire, speech, manner, and behavior. Aside from the obvious consideration of threshold appearance, it is important that Mr. Prospect see you at the very least in a neutral light. That is to say, you—the total man—should reflect the grooming and decorum that would minimize your becoming a negative factor in the selling situation. This, in actuality, is no small order. The fact is, we can easily offend or make others uncomfortable by our pattern of speech, quality of dress, living style, or a hundred and one other less obvious ways. What is so distressing about this is that few of us are aware of ourselves as possible negative sales factors. For some obscure reason, we assume that the prospect likes us and accepts us without corroborating the evidence to this effect. Few will come right out and tell you that you offend them or that they do not like you personally, but some will come mighty close to saying just that. To wit:

> One salesman was getting nowhere with a certain prospect and so he asked him, point blank, if he had anything against him personally. Mr. Prospect looked him in the eye and said, "Some men like Fords and others prefer Pontiacs. As for myself, I'm a Ford man and I see you as a Pontiac. Nothing can change that. . . ."

In the case above, the salesman took this intelligence to his manager; whereupon, a new salesman was assigned to this account. Shortly thereafter, he was seeing this new salesman as his "Ford man." But what of all the salesmen who fail their calling by whitewashing this selling impasse as the other guy's problem? Failing to see or report such selling intelligence is a very real handicap to many salesmen.

On the other hand, considering how Mr. Prospect thinks is a more discernible matter. You have no doubt heard the comment, ". . . it's not so much what the fellow said that bothered me, but the way he said it." Actually, what Mr. Prospect may mean is that he read in the salesman's remark an implication—a negative or derogatory insinuation. Though such an inference may be pure poppycock, his belief that you meant him ill can destroy the bridge to understanding. It is just possible that he understood from your remarks that you could see through his disguise; that you saw him naked as a man. To see through his pose is one thing; to fail to recognize and respect it, then, is quite another. Remember, we are not upset when there is no truth to what people say—only when there is a figment of truth or a hint of authenticity do we react. Keep this in mind. And above all, *never become personal*. Familiarity, indeed, tends to breed contempt in the sales situation. Too often flippancy takes form with familiarity. Hardly anything could be more damaging to the sales interview than this. Becoming personal or flippant are luxuries no salesman can afford. What is so difficult for many salesmen to realize is that Mr. Prospect is not interested in making friends, but simply in doing business. See him as a responsible businessman and he will reciprocate by seeing you as a man with whom he would do business. Friendship may grow out of your mutual business interests. Yet, it remains irrelevant as you attempt to convert him from a prospect into a customer. Avoid this faux pas by remembering this.

Fortunately, without Mr. Prospect saying a word, we can begin to develop a pretty reliable picture of the image he has of himself. It requires only that we utilize our God-given senses in a systematic manner:

1. What do you see?
2. What do you hear?
3. What do you observe?
4. What do you find or uncover?

A mirror image of the man can usually be created from this exploration.

Take his surroundings, for instance. They tend to reflect the inner man to a large degree. Where is his office located—near or removed from the seat of power? What books, magazines, or newspapers are in evidence? How are they arranged—neatly and impressively or haphazardly and obscurely? Do they appear to have been read? Make special note of the most worn, least worn books. Reflect on the content of these volumes. What do they tell you about the man? Theodore White, author of the *Making of the President* series, says that he would rather go through a man's library than through his wallet. Do you see pictures about? Are they of people, places, or things? Take special account of pictures of family, prominent men, or notable events. What do you see in them? What documents, certificates, and degrees are displayed? Collectively, what do they appear to mean? Are there lithographs, etchings, paintings, or prints in this room? Considering them in total, what effect do they produce? Later, check this against your impression of the man. How would you say his office is set up—for show or for work? Is it carpeted? What colors have been used? How would you describe his desk? Does it appear to be his working area or showpiece? Is it carefully and functionally arranged or is it a shambles? Would you say, then, that it reflects a man and a mind at work— unconscious and unconcerned about how others might see him? Does he have a desk calendar—does he appear to use it? Do you see anything unusual—something that doesn't seem to fit with the rest of the pattern? What do you make of all this? A word of caution: Don't be lulled into the idea that external order reflects internal order. On the contrary, a chaotic and desultory mind oftentimes would have a place for everything and everything in its place—in an attempt to hide from the reality of its confusion. Taking in Mr. Prospect's surroundings is done in an attempt to see him as he sees himself, nothing more.

Can you now appreciate how many ways he is trying to tell you who he is or who he thinks he is? Then too, something so slight as his modus operandi compared to his colleagues' can be quite revealing. For instance, a very dynamic and progressive individual in a staid and stuffy environment should cause you to wonder about this incongruity. Why do you suppose he is here? Is he family? Is he out to set this firm on its ear? Does he have authority? Let him tell you his story, in his own words. Wonder silently in your mind's eye. You would not be contributing to your purpose or his by making his "war" yours. In other words, address yourself to the area of your competence— the business of selling—armed, as it were, with this knowledge of him. This is sometimes a difficult course to follow —especially when he volunteers, "I don't know where to start. This place is so lethargic that it would make a Calvin Coolidge seem dynamic. Any suggestions, my friend?" It is at such a time that the salesman's courage is tested. The salesman should, at this juncture, communicate his real function and value to the prospect. An understanding of what the salesman can and cannot do should be clearly defined. What is more, those three reluctant words—*I don't know*—should find their way into the conversation, if indeed they are relevant. On the other hand, if the salesman is in fact selling a management consulting service or an allied program, this would be a most appropriate question. Should this be the case, the salesman must then decide whether the question is being proffered by the man in charge or by a disgruntled underling. Still, there is no reason to panic. The clues are there to lead you to the correct conclusion. They are revealed through your personal and environmental survey of Mr. Prospect. This is hidden somewhere in these factors:

1. Location of Mr. Prospect's office.
2. Furnishings of Mr. Prospect's office.
3. Appearance of Mr. Prospect's office.
4. Activity around Mr. Prospect's office.

Once the salesman is removed from the heat of the call, then he can take careful inventory of these observations and digest their significance. Sort impressions which are relevant to the man from those which are not. Now, how would you describe Mr. Prospect? Is he a fastidious man? A sloppy person? Is he fastidious in some respects and sloppy in others? Is he a doer more than a sayer, or the converse of this? Do you believe him? Do you trust him? Why? Don't use words or ideas that cloud your picture of him. You're trying to fill a blank canvas with a true portrait of the man you mean to sell. At the same time, don't be afraid to make note of looming inconsistencies.

Just as a painter may capture the kind eyes and cruel lips of his subject, the disparities observed in your subject, Mr. Prospect, should be faithfully recorded. To illustrate, he may swear like a trooper but be a deeply religious man. Or he may display the nervous energy of a ruthless despot, but appear to be surrounded by tranquil and happy subordinates. Or he may espouse to radical causes and ideas in the abstract, while reflecting a temperate demeanor in the concrete. Your job is to accept him as he is, taking pains to relate to the man he thinks he is, while embarrassing neither, as you attempt to meet the needs of both. To say that this is quite an order is an understatement. That is why you cannot afford a categorical or accidental approach to the sales situation.

Understanding the Three Levels
of Communication

Let us now continue our investigation of why. So often our minds are preoccupied with what we have to say that we don't hear Mr. Prospect. As a matter of fact, studies have been made to show that there are really three levels of hearing. These illustrate how poorly we listen:

1. There is the *hearing level*. We hear a noise and a muddled sound called talking but little else.

2. There is the *listening level*. We hear what a person is saying, but don't register his message.

3. There is the *thinking level*. We hear and understand the message of the person and properly digest its meaning.

Communication is only accomplished when we hit the third level. Developing the faculty for hearing with a "third ear" demands careful reflection, not to mention nearly flawless attention. Selling is one profession in which near perfection is required in communications. It is the backbone of the profession. In order for you to reply to a prospect's objections, statements, or doubts, they must, of course, be fully understood by you. That means that you must learn to listen. Even though listening is the other half of talking, it is evident that most of us are very poor listeners. This is not a shocking revelation. Have you ever wondered why we are such abominable listeners?

First of all, it is probably because listening isn't the simple thing it would seem to be. As pointed out above, it involves interpretation of both the literal meaning (meaning of the words or *explicit meaning*) as well as the intention of the speaker (implied meaning of the words or *implicit meaning*). If someone says, "Why, John, you old reprobate!", the words are practically an insult, but the tone of the speaker's voice probably indicates affection.

And secondly, there are several natural impediments to effective listening. A salesman may be easily affected by one or more of them. Consider these five possibilities:

1. *Distraction:* You are worried about a problem at home.
2. *Lack of Motivation:* Mr. Prospect takes too much time to get to the point.
3. *Wandering Mind:* You are thinking how you will spend the commission of a sale.
4. *Emotional Screen:* You actually can't stand Mr. Prospect.
5. *Rebuttal Instinct:* Mr. Prospect voices opinions that differ from yours.

A Checklist for Better Listening Habits

Since you are human, each of these will inevitably occur and prove more than tempting from time to time. Listening, to be sure, is demanding of that most rare human characteristic—self-discipline. See if this checklist doesn't aid you in acquiring better listening habits:

1. **Use Your Entire Body.** Utilize your eyes, ears, hands, and even your posture; show a real interest in what is being said in order to stimulate conversation. Surveys have shown that while 75% or more of communications we receive are verbal, and only 25% are written, the fact remains that only 15% of the information retained in our memories is received through the ears—the other 85% is received through the eyes.

2. **Give Mr. Prospect Your Absolute and Undivided Attention When He Talks.** This infers that you will not distract him with bodily movements, such as tapping the table with your finger or swaying from side to side.

3. **Don't Impose Your Will on Him.** Perhaps you are stronger, more quick-witted, dynamic, and confident than he is. Should you convey this to him by your expression or behavior in any way that is condescending, it will register with him. Consequently, his attitude may change towards you before the first word spills from your lips. Just as there are so many ways of losing the day with contemptible silence, there are tenfold as many opportunities to make Mr. Prospect feel important, vital, happy, warm, and in a word—comfortable. Why is it that some people, without so much as a word, exude so much warmth and charm? Try being like this to your

prospects and you won't believe the results. By your acceptance of them as they are, they will magnify your virtues and respond to your guidance.

4. **Don't Ever Argue.** All that is accomplished is that you stiffen his negative attitude towards you. This is another cause-effect relationship. Your respect and consideration of his point of view will gain you his admiration and loyalty. On the other hand, expose the fragility of his reason and you will win his contempt and hatred. The choice of friend or foe is clearly yours.

5. **Don't Make Him Feel Guilty.** Suppose he promised you an order, but failed to deliver on it. Let him explain. Give him the benefit of the doubt. From this graciousness you should be able to determine if it is a legitimate reason or not. Of course, if it turns out that it isn't, then he isn't really sold in the first place —is he?

6. **Avoid Destructive Talk.** You are told that a competitor of yours has come up with a brilliant idea. Your immediate reaction might be to neutralize this sudden intelligence quickly—this apparent advantage—by putting the competitor down. Of course, this action would accomplish quite the converse of this. So you would do well to take the news in good grace and share with Mr. Prospect his exuberant spirit, being careful to keep your sense of humor. Don't forget that he knows that his comment will needle you. Enjoy the game with him. It costs you nothing and probably brings you that much closer to the sale.

7. **Don't Monopolize the Presentation.** A sales call is a dialogue. His objections must have a complete airing, and total understanding must be realized before action can or will be taken.

To listen you must hear, understand, and display understanding. Train your mind not to race ahead planning your counterstatement. What more flattering gesture can you think of than for one to pause and ponder what you have said? Concentrate on your subject rather than your speech. Such detachment allows you to listen more analytically and to separate the words and their meanings. Don't let your mind pause to memorize the details of what has been said. You lose ground. Have confidence in your memory. It is not likely to let you down. Look for feeling behind what is said. Tone, inflection, facial expressions, bodily movements, and even breathing can give you a clue as to what Mr. Prospect is really thinking. Practice looking him in the eye when he talks to you, and you to him. Don't be surprised if he shows more trust and faith in you for this gesture. And finally, refrain from wishful listening. Don't put words you want to hear into his mouth. It may cause you much embarrassment later. If he says something which seems unlikely, check for understanding: ". . . excuse me, Mr. Prospect, I thought I heard you say . . ." If you have mistaken him, he will correct you.

Developing the Thinking Level of Communication

Since communication is such an important consideration in developing good understanding and since it is only accomplished when we hit the third level of hearing—the thinking level—it would be well to ask yourself these questions of Mr. Prospect:

1. **Are His Replies Concrete?** Or are they general, perhaps evasive? An evasive mood displayed in the opening of the call will unlikely change at the time of

closing. It also follows that a man who would talk in specifics, even about so mundane a subject as the weather, will indeed want to hear plenty of specifics from you.

2. **Does He Make Irrelevant Comments?** This is indicative of wandering attention. Remember, his attention is sensitive to promises of pleasure, excitement, or the solution of his problem. When you "romance" your sales presentation with the drama of fresh and tantalizing ideas, you fill him with the euphoria of expectation. Selling, then, in its most sophisticated essence, is tantamount to wooing—psychic solicitation.

3. **Does He Bring Up Objections Which Have Already Been Answered?** If he does, he either hasn't heard you or fails to understand your proffered explanation.

4. **What Kind of Words Does He Use?** How does he use them? Words are strong image indicators. If he fancies himself a technical expert and he's not, you would be wise to show him tolerance and respect in this discipline. Fitting this action to the situation might win him over immediately. You might just happen to be the first salesman demonstrating such kindness.

5. **Does He Visualize Well with Words?** Listen closely to how he states his views and his desires. Measure his facility for expressing himself against the complexity of your normal verbalizing. Then, tailor your presentation to language he will clearly understand. But extreme care should be taken, lest you become condescending.

6. **What Doesn't He Say?** His implicit meaning is conveyed in many ways. He may say, " . . . your program is twice as expensive as any other submitted,"

while he may actually mean, "I'll cut this whipper-snapper down to size. He wants this business. Let him beg for it." Should this be the case, you could be guilty of alienating him earlier in the call. Or it may simply be his way of testing you. Just as some people believe that anyone can be bought, there are those who believe a salesman can be pressured into cutting his price. In any event, check back and try to understand why.

7. **What About the Tone of His Voice?** High pitch may indicate tension. One's voice may also reveal decisiveness, insecurity, aggression, etc. Learn to associate his voice with his inherent disposition.

8. **What About His Listening Technique?** Is he courteously attentive or is he rudely preoccupied? Listening techniques reflect the psychology of his self-image. Measured speech, with controlled pauses after thinking about what you have said, is an index of good listening technique, not to mention a form of high compliment. What is more, it tells you that he accepts you and is responsive to your cause. It is precisely for this reason that we would do well to remember this when he has queried us.

Interruptions in sales interviews are a common experience. At first consideration this would hardly be judged a blessing. But think about it. What better opportunity does one have to apply the sum and substance of this discussion than to observe Mr. Prospect at work? His involvement in work supplies us with actions which either support or belie his words. They give us a kaleidoscopic view of his projected self-image. Let us study him for a moment to better understand this:

1. **What kind of person is he?** Is he a tyrant demanding

action from his subordinates or does he appear to treat them all like men?

2. And his supervisors—do they seem relaxed and self-assured? Does he deal with them as he does his other subordinates? How do they treat him?

3. And his peers—does he get on with them?

4. And the distaff side of his office—does he treat them like ladies? How do they treat him?

5. And his superiors—does he seem as natural with them as he is with his other associates?

6. And phone calls—does he answer formally or casually; does he display forcefulness and dispatch or does he waver; does he use the call to impress you; does he seem to have a distinct telephone personality?

7. Is his office open and available to all callers?

8. Does he seem to take interruptions in stride?

This may seem a bit too involved to be worthwhile—but is it? Actually, there are scores of questions which might be expected to bombard a curious mind while observing. In fact, a good salesman develops a complex, if not conscious, eclectic system for taking measure of his prospect's personality and buying mood of the moment. All that is being suggested here is that this process be given some order and forethought so that it may be controlled and used with the greatest facility and efficacy. Such an exercise, to be sure, takes only seconds to employ, but perhaps hours to perfect. Yet once learned, the correct data can be fed to your computer-like brain for an accurate and meaningful appraisal. That is to say, you will consider everything your senses tell you as either relevant or irrelevant to establishing understanding with Mr. Prospect. Time is only a factor while you are acquiring this skill. Once acquired, though, you are ahead of 80% of your professional colleagues.

If you have deduced from this discussion that what one buys is mainly dictated by emotion, rather than reason, you are correct. Given two products of a similar quality, the salesman tapping the prospect's buying impulse, his emotion if you will, comes out the contest winner in no less than eight out of 10 cases. So this probing technique, which is the basis of this study, is actually designed to provide you with a better chance of uncovering or finding, and then exploiting, Mr. Prospect's emotional need(s). There are several practical methods of accomplishing this end:

1. **Capitalize on Emotion-Evoking Topics.** Suppose you comment on the building going on in his area. His reply may give you a clue as to how he feels about progress, change, confusion, disorder, competition, or newness.

2. **Provoke a Discussion of Benefits and What They Mean to Him.** Get him to relate the benefits he looks for in a product, service, company, and representative of the ilk that you have to offer.

3. **Ask Him to Comment on Your Program or Service.** Don't be afraid to say, "Mr. Prospect, now that you have heard about our program, how would you compare it to your present one?" Ask him what he thinks is really needed. This makes him focus attention on your program. At the same time, it gives him an opportunity to make positive statements. You are both working together to solve a problem—his problem. In this manner, you demonstrate that you have his best interests at heart while you are showing him what is in it for him.

4. Spot the Clues His Objections Give. If it is price, plunge forward by saying, "Mr. Prospect, you seem very much concerned about the price of this program. Am I correct in assuming that it is the operating costs which really bother you?" Perhaps he is a bargainer and fears paying too much. Allay his misgivings, then pursue your advantage. Educate him as to the true nature of costs and what the real savings to him will be.

5. Think. Use your total experience, imagination, and intuition to explore those areas revealed by your probing. Leave no stone unturned. Keep reminding yourself that in many ways we are all alike. Emotional drives which appear to govern him also operate in us as well. Only the intensity of these drives differs from person to person. You are advised to gauge Mr. Prospect's drives always in the light of this fact.

This has been a strenuous exercise, no doubt as much for the reader as the author. So if you feel a bit weary, it is certainly understandable. Unquestionably, in trying to understand Mr. Prospect, you have become more involved in yourself. *This is significant.* When someone confounds us, we tend to think in terms of ourselves as well as in terms of our confounder in order to perceive motivation. In other words, we might use ourselves as the reference point for establishing understanding with others. As a salesman you should never lose sight of this. Wrapped up in each individual is actually the body, mankind. Selling might take this into account. On the other hand, what Mr. Prospect may need and want could be worlds apart. Your job, then, is to make him want that which he needs. Sometimes this requires the patience and understanding of a God.

SELF-STUDY QUESTIONS:

Think carefully before answering the following questions. All affirmative answers should be accompanied by a brief explanation. True or false:

1. Outer poise reflects an inner calm.
2. Very bright women tend to be quite unattractive.
3. Slow workers invariably are more careful.
4. People always say what they mean.
5. People always say what they feel.
6. Silent men usually are deep thinkers.
7. People smile at you when they like you.

Consider these questions below and imagine the questioner. What does it reveal to you about him?

1. Why is Tom such a show-off?
2. Why do the Smiths spend more money than they make?
3. Tell me, why was Norm given that promotion?
4. Why does Harry always shrink from responsibility?
5. Why is Ted so touchy?
6. Can you understand why Frank is such an apple polisher?

Note: *This exercise is meant to have you listen with the third ear.*

RECOMMENDED FURTHER READING:

Eric Berne, M.D. *Games People Play* (Grove Press, 1964).

Smiley Blanton, M.D. *Love or Perish* (Simon and Schuster, 1956).

Harry Emerson Fosdick. *On Being a Real Person* (Harper & Row, 1943).

Edward T. Hall, Ph.D. *The Silent Language* (Fawcett Publications, Inc., 1959).

Eric Hoffer. *The True Believer* (Harper & Row, 1951).

Vernon Howard. *Your Magic Power to Persuade and Command People* (Prentice-Hall, Inc., 1962).

Kenneth S. Keyes, Jr. *How to Develop Your Thinking Ability* (McGraw-Hill Book Company, Inc., 1950).

Donald A. Laird and Eleanor C. Laird, Ph.D., Sc.D. *The Technique of Handling People* (McGraw-Hill Book Company, Inc., 1943, 1954).

Maxwell Maltz, M.D., F.I.C.S. *The Magic Power of Self-Image Psychology* (Prentice-Hall, Inc., 1964).

William L. McCaskill. *How to Get Through to People in Selling* (Parker Publishing Company, Inc., 1970).

Stuart Palmer. *Understanding Other People* (Fawcett Publications, Inc., 1964).

Theodor Reik, Ph.D. *Listening with the Third Ear* (Pyramid Publications, Inc., 1964).

Dagobert D. Runes. *The Art of Thinking* (Philosophical Library, Inc., 1961).

Larry S. Skurnik and Frank George. *Psychology for Every Man* (Penguin Books, Inc., 1964).

Baruck Spinoza. *How to Improve Your Mind* (The Citadel Press, 1962).

Robert H. Thouless. *How to Think Straight* (Hart Publishing Company, Inc., 1932).

(4) Overcoming Common Obstacles to Success— The Power of Skillful Persuasion

Thus far, we have established that the salesman is, himself, the most common, if not the principal, obstacle to successful selling. And that only by knowing and understanding his own personal attitudes can the salesman expect to succeed with a cross section of his prospects. This notwithstanding, you may still be wishing all kinds of doom or misfortune for your intransigent prospects. Even as you read this, you might be thinking:

> I can hardly wait for that hard-head, Mr. Smith, to retire or drop dead. Why not? I can't sell him and I'm betting you couldn't either. No one can sell that old relic. And no words are going to convince me otherwise!

True, words will not uncoil your fixation. But I'm betting your sense of fair play and reason will turn the trick. Now think for a moment. Is this predisposition really fair or reasonable to assume by either you or Mr. Smith? Certainly you are not selling to him, but apparently someone else has him tied up. On this point there should be no debate. Hopefully, when you have completed this chapter, you will have a better insight into why he is buying elsewhere, as well as a new strategy for changing this situation.

Admittedly, pure hustle and extensive canvassing will bring you in a number of new customers. But when you run out of "yes men," as all of us do sooner or later, then what do you do? Pressure tactics which are designed to wear the "no men" down usually prove futile in the end. As a matter of fact, often they produce a very hostile climate and give you and your company a bad name. Therefore, you would do well to avoid putting overt pressure on Mr. Prospect. Instead, the more subtle art, persuasion, might be employed to circumvent these difficulties. This is not always an easy chore.

Take the average new salesman, for example. He feels that he must be brilliant to be believed and everything to everybody to sell. His most natural inclination is to immerse himself in product technology and company know-how to the exclusion of his professional development as a salesman. This is his penchant, not necessarily the preference of his employer. Nevertheless, he does this sincerely believing that he is putting first things first; that he is tackling the more difficult phase of his job first. This thinking is fine, except for one cardinal flaw. All the job knowledge in the world will avail him nothing if he cannot get through to people. All this preparation will be for naught if he cannot recognize and measure Mr. Prospect's buying mood. You cannot expect Mr. Prospect to have the same doubts and misgivings as you; nor to think or reason with the same logic. What would appeal to a logical, analytical person, therefore, may not generate the interest of a dreamy, abstract individual. In the same respect, a person who thinks in shades of gray would hardly appreciate being overwhelmed by a black and white presentation. Nor would a prospect of rigid mental discipline be moved to anything but disgust by a sales story tied loosely together in non sequiturs. Nor would an austere and aloof salesman come on very strong to a warm and affable prospect, unless he relaxes a bit.

Fortunately, in learning the art of persuasion, it is necessary to cultivate discernment at the expense of rote selling —a case where a positive eliminates a negative aspect.

The problem of getting through to people is really quite intriguing. As people, for instance, it interests us "to know what makes the other guy tick." The knowing, to be sure, is difficult because our minds seldom meet—and then, only fleetingly. Why, would you imagine? The problem appears to stem from two rather obvious sources:

1. Being human ourselves.

2. Forgetting that others are human.

Can you picture how easy it would be if all your prospects were mechanical robots? There would be no pre-existing attitudes which might conflict with your ideas; no emotions to distract your prospects from your intended purpose; no fragile egos to stroke. Then again, you would probably become quite bored with it all in a very short time. The entire situation would be too predictable. Missing would be the sense of challenge and the taste of victory.

But you needn't worry. Man remains elusive. What is more, as evidence of this fact, a veritable "tug-of-war" continues unabated. This mental struggle between reason and unconscious need operates within every man, acting, as it were, as a constant threat to straight thinking, clear communications, and a meeting of the minds.

Four Keys to Human Tendencies

Let us begin this exercise by examining some human tendencies and analyze how they may possibly interfere with our getting through to others:

1. **We Tend to Resist Change.** We are all creatures of habit. Every thought, feeling, and action is influenced by habit. But contrary to what you may think, repetition of an act is not sufficient incentive to make it a habit. In addition to repeating it, there must be some clear-cut gain in doing it. This gain or benefit makes us more comfortable and self-assured. Consequently, we are reluctant to give it up; we are reluctant to change. That is why an advantage or benefit must be clearly evident in trying something new. Mr. Prospect may have promised you he would give you his next order. He likes you and has faith in your ability. Yet, the time comes and goes only to find him failing to keep his word. Is he a liar, a procrastinator, or is he simply afraid to change? As mentioned before, it is well to give him the benefit of the doubt. Perhaps he sees himself only as he is and not as you would have him be. In other words, he cannot visualize or see himself using your program. He may say to himself, "These sophisticated new products must be good or this young man wouldn't be selling them. Still, they are really beyond me. And if I can't

90

fathom how they work, how can I expect my men to understand? No, much as I'd like to give this fellow a try, I just can't accept the risk. I'll have to tell him next time he comes in." This is a serious matter to him. Change means becoming another man, wearing another hat. It means taking off the uniform of a supervisor and putting on the garb of a teacher, an engineer. What might you do to save the day? One approach you may consider would involve anticipating his dilemma. Then, like a perceptive clothier, you ease him into a new "suit of clothes" by showing him how much better off he is for having made the change. Paint him a positive verbal picture: "Mr. Prospect, I can see you now. With the establishment of this program, you'll have more time to make those repairs you've been planning. And besides, you can take that vacation you've been promising yourself. This program is a complete package and it is so simple that you needn't worry about special training for your men. Let me explain . . ."

2. **We Tend to Prefer Thinking Our Own Thoughts.** Have you ever noticed how difficult it is to remain attentive when someone else is speaking? Your mind races ahead as your computer brain jumps frantically from one circuit to another. Meanwhile, the spoken word lopes along at a snail's pace. Consequently, only a presentation that is brisk, lean, and sparkling has a chance. At the same time, it must be couched in the idiom of the prospect and presented at the cadence of his thinking. Otherwise, you will lose him before you have him. Remember, if he seems to be a slow thinker, take pains to check his understanding of your sales story, point by point. On the other hand, should he possess a razor-sharp mind, don't labor unnecessarily at a boring pace, but get to the essence

91

of your ideas. When his mind still wanders off, despite these efforts, bring him back with a courteous comment: "Mr. Prospect, let us dispense with these technical details. You're primarily interested in results. These are the results you can expect . . ." Knowing "key" words which appeal to him is invaluable as a device for increasing and then sustaining his attention. His receptivity for such words as new, trouble-free, proven, and lifesaver will furnish you with clues as to his propensity. It is also possible to gauge his attention by these already discussed signs:

a. He asks unnecessary questions.

b. He makes irrelevant comments.

c. He brings up objections already disposed of.

(You will remember these from the discussion in the last chapter on the third ear.) Then, again, your attention may also wander. In that case, a very simple physical gesture may bring you quickly back—namely, replenishing your oxygen supply by taking a deep breath. This clears your head. Once you are yourself again, you may ask Mr. Prospect to repeat his last statement in an appropriate manner: "Pardon me, sir, would you mind repeating your last remark?" Please note that your concentration will be materially assisted if you have a well-conceived sales call plan. This will aid you in maintaining control of the interview. Incidentally, by control I do not mean to suggest that you dominate the talking. Later you will be shown how silence can be used most effectively to accomplish this purpose.

3. **We Tend to Prefer Hearing What We Want to Hear.** "Everyone views life through rose-colored glasses." This idea was put to song and verse some years ago. "Wishes are the dreams we dream when we're awake," was how the lyric went. Certainly, it

is not difficult to picture a salesman in this puzzled clime: "Mr. Prospect, I was nearly certain that I heard you say 30 cases. Not 30 cartons!" It is so easy for our aspirations to get in the way of our correct hearing. This, in itself, provides the best possible reason for the cold appraisal or critique after the sales call—post-call analysis, if you prefer. Never again will everything be so fresh in your mind. Then too, if you don't develop the practice of writing down the pertinent details of the call immediately following it, chances are you never will. These invaluable gems of information will be lost forever, literally written on the wind. To justify this desultory conduct, there is the great temptation to tell yourself, "Nothing spectacular happened anyway. I will remember what's worthwhile remembering." Sure you will! How many times have you been reminded by a superior, peer, customer, or prospect of promises not kept? One need only consult his own company's purchasing staff to learn how frequently salesmen repeat the same promises, call after call, without ever delivering. Feeble excuses only make matters worse. The fact remains that somewhere along the line the salesman has forgotten, as we all do from time to time. More than likely, he has failed to write it down. Why? Perhaps he has not been sufficiently motivated; perhaps he has failed to see the inherent benefit to him. Accepting this as a possibility, let us decide right now to give this idea a trial run of one month's duration. I promise you that before the month is out you will note a new aura of efficiency. You will discover new pleasures in being taken and accepted at your word. Suddenly, you will note the gradual building towards a close of your more difficult prospects as each call becomes synergized by the previous calls. You will happily take up where you left off; no longer will you have to start each call from scratch. You will find yourself, for perhaps the first time, getting off the treadmill of repeating the same mistakes each call, mistakes which doubtless have cost you dearly in sales not made. With a record in front of you, a history of your sales activity, new strategies will come to mind for future sales situations—based, as it were, on what has worked in the past. And finally, a pattern will begin to unfold, exposing your operational, if not personal, strengths and weaknesses. At the same time, you note prospect types that are the easiest—most difficult—for you to close. Essentially, then, you will be arriving at a much truer perspective or profile of your sales activity/sales proficiency. At what sacrifice?—only five minutes of reflection and note taking after each call. So begin this practice at once; repeat it religiously. One month from today you will be able to look back on impressive gains. And in these gains, hopefully, a new habit will be born.

4. **We Tend to Victimize Ourselves with False or Unwarranted Assumptions.** Turn your imagination on! Picture yourself calling on your favorite account. Now, think of yourself making a similar call on your competitor's favorite account. Can you see yourself walking confidently and happily into your account, but quite meekly and apologetically into his? Why? Let us add one more dimension to this hypothetical situation. Imagine your competitor knowing all the weak points in your account; that is, areas of possible vulnerability from people, places, or things. Would you, with such knowledge, be able to strut as confidently into your account? Would you feel terror? Why? This, incidentally, illustrates one of the biggest reasons why some make it and some don't. A salesman and his personality, insofar as Mr. Prospect is con-

cerned, are wrapped in the essence of his assumptions. Assume that he will buy, and he will buy; assume that he is out to get you, and get you he will; assume that he is glad to see you, and he will greet you with open arms. If only a salesman would walk into each prospect's office as confidently and expectantly as he would his favorite account; then no one could deny him. But once again, it is a case of easier said than done. By exploring the why of this behavior, perhaps a step can be taken towards making more of our assumptions positive and true reflections of the facts as they exist. Knowing and understanding breed confidence. You sense that you are appreciated and recognized when you have know-how. Moreover, you assume that you are accepted for what you are, and that your company —its products, programs, and services—is duly recognized as well. This builds eagerness, enthusiasm, and anticipation. The warmth of your personality draws others into the sphere of your influence naturally, spontaneously. On the other hand, your charm, sincerity, and affability are likely to desert you when the ground is not familiar, or is considered hostile. One's whole behavior, under the circumstances, is apt to be stilted. Far from giving yourself an even chance, you contribute to your competitor's cause, if not his security, by showing yourself in the worst possible light. Why? This is difficult to perceive. It has been my experience that veteran salesmen are as guilty of this faux pas as the new recruit. This, incidentally, is the major reason the beginner puts knowledge above all else. He sees himself a naked and negative entity before customer and prospect alike. At the same time, the veteran may have a large sense of guilt or fear— guilt in that he doesn't know or understand what he should; fear in that competition will see through his fragile defenses, his poor selling. In fact, were the veteran to assume that competition "knew something" —something that might jeopardize his hold on his accounts—his whole being would likely reflect his terror. This, of course, is uncalled for. If each man, be he recruit or veteran, is doing the best job he can, there is no reason to worry. No one can ask any more of a man. But herein lies the paradox. Generally speaking, the salesman, not the forces or people outside, victimizes himself with false or unwarranted assumptions. These assumptions are costly errors in judgment and can be very emotionally distressing for anyone who has difficulty putting them in their proper perspective.

A Checklist for Offsetting Invalid Assumptions

A checklist is offered to mollify this difficulty:

a. Never assume anyone is competent until he proves it to you. Don't judge another by what a third party says.

b. Make certain everyone in your account who has influence knows you and what you are doing for him.

c. Use your knowledge of your customer's operation to conceive what possible problems your competitor's accounts may have. Probe the advantage of this perception. Never accept the answer, "We are happy. We have no problems."

d. Don't assume anyone knows more about your business—be it product, program, service, or technology —than you. This is not a license for arguing, but certainly a reason to be confident.

e. Don't talk down, up, or at people, but with them. If you feel any of these tendencies, examine the situation. Are you guilty of unwarranted or false assumptions?

f. Walk into a prospect's office with the idea, "I can help him. I will help him."

g. Think: I have my customer's/prospect's best interests at heart.

h. Should you feel panic or fear moving in on you, wait! It will pass. Be patient! Your poise will bring your confidence back.

i. Don't argue, but reflect a prospect's bad manners back to him: "You say we are con artists?" The sting of his own words should cool him.

j. Do your very best each call. This will build your competence as it gives you confidence. You may then assume most assuredly he will buy, and that he will be happy with what he has bought.

k. If a complaint is lodged against you and/or your company, don't assume the defensive. Hear the complaint, investigate it, and then resolve it in a manner which would have the facts of the case speak for themselves.

We tend to cloak ourselves in habitual secretiveness. The meeting of the minds is truly hampered when this is the problem. Some people desire to literally hide "in themselves" for fear of disclosure. Motivation for this may spring from a lack of confidence or an insufficient sureness of one's thoughts. Apparently, people of such inclination feel a need to hide these thoughts from view. But why they would do this to themselves can only be speculated. Some have suggested it is because they have a basic contempt for their own views. Feeling so, they are apt to suspect or fear that others—if they only knew of these thoughts, of this secret scorn and terror they harbored within—would have contempt for them. Not surprising, then, this type of person does not exercise discretion. That is to say, he maintains a cloak of secrecy over everything, no matter what it is he is talking about, or to whom he might be speaking. In his mind this is a necessary safety precaution. At first thought, you may consider this an altogether far too infrequent human tendency to justify inclusion in this discussion. Moreover, you may find this accounting too clinical. Frankly, I was once of a similar mind. In sheer quantitative terms, it is, indeed, a proclivity seldom uncovered. But when you do confront it, such statistics are of little help or solace. It has been my personal experience to find this "tight-lipped corps" snugly ensconced in trusted positions in management and government, as well as in professional and educational institutions. And I have met men of this ilk with increasing frequency as my own career has advanced. Make no mistake, he is out there. If you haven't met him yet, you will. It behooves you, therefore, to understand him, for his influence may very well have either a direct or indirect bearing on a buying decision. It is imperative that you recognize and cultivate him. Trust, though difficult to establish, is probably the most direct route to winning him. The subsequent case history illustrates how one salesman tackled this problem. It is a progress report of this young man to his manager, disclosing his exhilaration at finally having a meeting of the minds with Mr. Secret.

THE REPORT: Mr. Secret Exposed

"This represents one of the most rewarding days of my selling career. And mind you, I didn't get the order. Permit me to explain.

When I first met Mr. Secret over two years

ago, I recognized he had a deep-seated contempt for us. So prejudiced was his attitude that a climate to sell was virtually nonexistent. I shall never forget that first call. Ted (the man whom this salesman was replacing) had made an appointment with Mr. Secret to introduce me and to let him know that I would be calling on him. To start off, he gave me a limp hand to shake and then failed to look me in the eye. As a matter of fact, he never looked me in the eye before today. Instead, he spun his chair around and gave Ted and I his back to view. He also kept himself occupied clipping his nails, paying neither of us even the slightest heed. This display of rudeness alarmed and embarrassed us both. I remember Ted apologizing to me after the call. It was apparent that Mr. Secret had even outdone himself in this affront. I wondered why—why today? My curiosity was more stimulated than my concern. I knew I would have to find out why he hated us so; why he would show us his ugliest side. There just had to be a reason. One thing was certain. I couldn't get anywhere with him as matters now stood.

The situation called for a long-term Master Plan. For such a plan to work it was going to have to be subtle, imaginative, and well executed. I was going to have to use all my guns. Next, there was the matter of time. This was difficult to judge. Optimism dictated that all my goals should be achieved in one year. Results to date prove I was quite a bit off. Actually, I have revised this plan many times in the past two years. Here is my original plan:

　1. Give of myself. Put him in the center of my interest as well as concern.

2. Know the man—his thoughts, his attitudes, his desires, and his needs.

3. Seek rapport. Make him feel at ease and comfortable; show him love, trust, and charity; develop a favorable climate to sell.

4. Assay his attitude towards me and my company; determine if he harbors a personal grudge; study his loyalty to his present suppliers.

5. Advance his thinking to encompass the role we can play in his operation.

6. Allow him to select *his* program.

To accomplish the first step of this plan, I had to prepare myself mentally. Many times I had to bite my lip as he resorted to ways of antagonizing me. But oddly enough, he would always see me. I gave him the benefit of the doubt for this. Gradually, my concern for self receded and my interest in him became truly genuine. At about the same time he stopped playing the 'heavy.'

I found I couldn't really get to know the man at the plant, so I decided to ask him to lunch. That started a series of long luncheon breaks with most interesting results. He was, to be sure, reluctant at first to engage in these private conversations. After awhile, however, he seemed to look forward to them with marked anticipation. We would discuss psychology, philosophy, current events, history, and other cerebral subjects. He admitted to having a thirst for knowledge. But I saw a hunger for expression, appreciation, and a sense of value as well. I would listen and contribute sparingly. Occasionally, I would feel guilty for not pressing. Yet, even the slightest reference to business would cause him to freeze. That is when I decided on a slightly new tack: I chose not to mention business at all. This had a marked effect upon Mr. Secret. You could tell, after awhile, that he was waiting for the pitch. When it didn't come, he looked somewhat defeated; as if he needed to reassure himself that he was still in charge. A 'Pavlov reflex' had been seeded.

With no pressure being exerted, on the other hand, there was no need for him to assume the defensive, no need for him to be anyone but himself. Gradually, in an oblique manner, comments were woven into the fabric of the conversation which were responsive to his more relaxed mood: 'Did you see that article in Business Week on a new material we are placing on the market?' Each time this was done, less and less suppressed resentment was noted. His comments, nevertheless, remained succinct and noncommittal. And I might add that they were not challenged either.

This brings us to the fourth step of the Master Plan which we accomplished today—two years later. Heartened by a well-received presentation —he admitted our technology was on the move— I mustered the courage to ask, 'Mr. Secret, what do you really think of my company?' He was obviously taken back by this question. But he did not go into his freeze. Instead, he stared deep into my eyes and then seemingly took forever to reply. Finally, he said, 'A few years ago your company's big shots royally entertained my boss at a technical meeting. He came back and nonchalantly mentioned this, asking me to take a look at you when I had the time. Then, before I could catch my breath, your pressure boys swarmed in on me. I felt like I had had a plunger forced down my throat. You can certainly imagine how it made me feel.' Then, he paused and smiled triumphantly, adding, 'I'll bet somebody caught hell in your home office for losing this plum!'

It was finally out. At last he had gotten it off his chest. Seeming somewhat embarrassed by his vindictive admission, however, he assuaged by suggesting, 'I think you would have felt the same way I did.' Of course, I concurred. Taking advantage of his solicitous mood, but being careful not to offend him, I then developed a picture of a 'new company,' a company with which he would be pleased to work, a company tailored to meet his needs. I began to lay the groundwork for his future conversion to us. I have achieved a foothold on step five of my Master Plan and I think it will be only a matter of time, now, before this $200,000 account is mine . . ."

Mr. Secret is admittedly an unusual problem, if not a surprising study in sales strategy, but the potential indicates that this salesman's efforts were worthwhile. You're not convinced? Perhaps you are thinking, "This guy had the patience of Job, but come now, was he really selling or just dogging it?" This raises a more significant question: Does a salesman have to come away with the order to consider his call a success? It is my contention that he doesn't. By that I simply mean, each call should either bring you the order or closer to it. Every football play is diagrammed to go for a touchdown. Yet, a coach is happy to see his team make only a first down because it brings them that much closer to a score. Selling is quite analogous to this.

What's more, in the case of Mr. Secret, you must think of this salesman's alternatives. Circumventing Mr.

Secret had created animosity and rigidity, while it became apparent that overt pressure justified Mr. Secret's open hostility towards this salesman's company. Developing a Master Plan for his prospect gave this salesman a diagram —a guide, if you will—to what had to be done, and a gauge to the progress made in that direction.

Techniques for Gaining Skill in Persuasion

You should now have a fair appreciation as to why a meeting of the minds is difficult. Let us then consider techniques for dealing with these human factors of behavior. Acquiring skill in persuasion will require a good deal of practice. Likewise, you will only benefit from these suggestions if you try to apply them to real situations. In doing this, you will find the bridge to mutual understanding is not a one-way thoroughfare. That is, if you intelligently analyze the problem and take the first step in this direction, you will find Mr. Prospect willing to more than meet you halfway. As you read the following Eight-Point Plan for getting through to others, think of your most troublesome prospects:

1. **Encourage Cooperation.** Conversation is the salesman's principal vehicle for expressing ideas. He uses this device to subject his prospects to two influences: *logic* and *emotional need satisfaction.* Responsiveness to these influences varies, from individual to individual. But you must recognize that they exist. And, then, you should develop a talent for dealing with each prospect on an individual basis.

   You have progressed a long way when you realize that you cannot rely on logic alone. This often proves a difficult hurdle for the salesman to overcome, especially the technical salesman. A natural inclination is to fill the air with precise and sometimes pompous detail to the bafflement of Mr. Prospect. What should be uppermost in your mind, namely, his goodwill and cooperation, can easily get lost in your zeal to sell. Simple courtesy is a fine starter in the direction of winning his cooperation. And you demonstrate this when you see that your prospect gains something from his conversation with you.

Should this seem too obvious to mention, you might check to see if you are hitting these three important bases every call:

a. State the purpose of your call: "Mr. Prospect, I would like to show you how our program can reduce your production costs by 40%." Your clarity, directness, and honesty will likely establish a body of trust, not to mention arouse his buying interests.

b. Observe the prospect's mood. If he seems preoccupied and a bit weary, you might say, "Mr. Prospect, apparently I've caught you on a real hectic day. Would you like me to reschedule my call for another time?" If, indeed, you have judged the situation correctly, he will be deeply grateful to you for your thoughtfulness. If you have misread things, he will still appreciate your concern and remember you for it. In either case, you gain.

c. Allow the prospect to become comfortable. This may mean listening to an irrelevancy or two at the beginning of the call. Perhaps he has just left a budget meeting and feels exhausted, even crushed. To compensate for this experience he might begin by telling you how good he is, or how he isn't really appreciated. By accepting and allowing him this emotional release, you substantially improve your chances of getting him to react favorably to you in the end.

2. **Draw Out Your Prospect's Thoughts.** Think of this a moment. Your job requires that you draw information from your prospect. In other words, you are putting a demand on him to do something for you—to give up time, and energy, and possibly information that he does not, in fact, wish to reveal. Does it sound foreboding? It shouldn't. And interestingly enough, it won't if you make the giving an enjoyable experience for him.

Expressing your appreciation and listening with interest to his comments are two thoughtful ways of accomplishing just that.

It is also most considerate of you if the questions you ask are carefully framed for easy answering. What's more, they should be designed for full and accurate information. For instance, once he appears comfortable and, of course, receptive, you might ask: "What is your daily production?" This kind of query calls for a specific fact. Little thinking is required of the prospect.

A more effective way of drawing out information, however, requires Mr. Prospect to talk about a particular topic rather than a specific fact. Here are a few possible ways of achieving that objective:

    a. Ask questions which cannot be answered with a "YES" or "NO":
      What do you think about our program?
      How do you measure production costs?

105

How do you feel about making the change?
What benefits do you need?
What benefits do you expect?

b. Preface key words with "what about" or "how about":
What about control?
What about safety?
How about the convenience of service?
How about the economy of a packaged program?
What about savings?

c. Repeat back key words that happen to be of a negative nature. For instance:
Prospect: You've got a good product but it's too high.
You: Too high?
This is asking Mr. Prospect to explain what he means by "too high." Perhaps he is thinking in terms of price per pound and has failed to consider the actual cost—the cost performance of the product, service, and/or program.

d. Summarize back: "Mr. Prospect, let me see if I understand you correctly. You like our program but feel it would be more expensive than your present system. Is that correct?" Then, you show him the real costs of your program and the actual savings he will realize by converting to it.

3. **Deal with the Prospect's Emotions.** This has been the common theme threading its way through this entire book. In my selling career, I have found a great need for an insight into emotions—mine as well as Mr. Prospect's. I have failed to find the answers in selling books and have found myself, over the years,

turning more and more to psychology and, yes, philosophical tomes for the answers. Doubtlessly, they have helped. They have given me some insight and direction, but nothing I have ever read matches the psychological drama of the actual selling situation. Buying and selling are conducted in an absolute atmosphere of emotion. No matter how coldly logical a prospect may be, reason is momentarily abandoned when he says "yes" and signs the order. He has, in effect, surrendered to the will of another man. In a word, he has been seduced. There is just no plainer way of putting it. Never in my selling career have I seen this last step transpire otherwise. Parenthetically speaking, this is not to be construed as suggesting that there is one magic emotional moment when Mr. Prospect may be closed. There are literally scores of opportunities in every sales call to tap his emotional reserve. Know that all of us are controlled by emotion when we buy—no matter what the product, service, or situation may be. Sophisticated dialectics or shrewd chicanery aside, emotion holds the key to the lock on every final door—the door to close. Use this key wisely and it will serve you well. Much of your anxiety and frustration, not to mention fear, will vanish when this key is adroitly applied.

To assist you to this end, it is helpful to consider emotion as essentially a motivator. Building on this premise, it follows that the key to putting Mr. Prospect in a buying mood depends to a large degree on how effectively you recognize and then utilize his particular set of motivators. Let us now examine some common motivational factors:

> a. **Character or Value System.** This is a fundamental view of your prospect. Everything he says and does is salient to this factor. His

comments regarding politics, religion, beliefs, his fellow workers, world, immediate community, and personal values reflect the quality, if not the propensity, of the inner man in question.

b. **Interests.** You will observe by his behavior and attitude whether he is work or play oriented. Moreover, you will have many clues as to how he enjoys his work. For instance, ask yourself: Does the job match the man? Are the job and man compatible? Does the man seem bent on pursuing *his* interests?

c. **Aspirations.** Everyone is a dreamer to some degree. No doubt your prospect has a fond dream tucked away in his memory. Make no mistake, identify your program with his repressed, if not expressed, desires and you are well on your way to a sale.

d. **Status-Striving Drive.** Keep always in mind that each of us seeks the approval of others so that we may in turn approve of ourselves. That is essentially what the drive for status is all about—that is, an interest in appearing favorably in the eyes of others. If you can identify the prospect's self-image and relate to it in your selling, you will enhance his buying mood and immeasurably improve your chances of closing.

e. **Security.** No one escapes the grasp of this emotional factor. He who would deny it is its greatest slave. A perception of security governs everyone. Some measure of this can be gleaned by carefully studying Mr. Prospect. Often, a tendency to be defensive or sarcastic is a red-lettered banner signaling insecurity. Key words go a long way in soothing the insecure prospect: Such words as "safer," "well-serviced," "controlled," "insurance," and "proven" have been shown to be effective in this regard.

There are, of course, many other human motivators which could be included in this listing. In each case, the mechanics are the same. You look past the man you see before you to the whole person, including the man inside. In other words, you see Mr. Prospect doing a job and wonder why he does it and what satisfaction he derives from doing it. Then, you reflect on how you might make his job more fulfilling, not to mention less a burden to him. You can do all this by appealing and then dealing effectively with his human emotions.

This takes us to the how step of dealing with Mr. Prospect's emotions. The following are three time-tested approaches you might consider:

a. **Encourage Expression.** Picture yourself calling on a disgruntled customer. This man has a tremendous temper. And besides, you know that the fault lies with his people and not your company at all. How would you handle him? Consider the effect of this possible question:

> "Mr. Customer, I understand you're unhappy with our service. Would you please explain the difficulty to me?"

Wouldn't his anger be somewhat placated by this gesture? Once he has gotten it off his chest, he will remember what a hard time he has given you.

b. Make Him Aware of His Own Feelings.
Now, if your prospect or customer is still
in a hostile mood after answering your question, you might say:

> "Mr. Customer, you appear to have
> taken this whole matter very per-
> sonally. Have we offended you?
> Have I?"

This would force your man to examine his
own feelings more closely to see whether
or not this is, indeed, true.

**c. Accept His Emotions Without Criticizing
Them.** Once Mr. Customer has weighed
his wrath, it is not uncommon for him to
show discomfort and to become apologetic.
This gives you an excellent opportunity to
reassure him:

> "Sir, I certainly can understand your
> reason for being upset with our serv-
> ice. I've got an idea how it might be
> improved. Would you like to hear
> it?"

Does all this sound pretty simple? You
might even be thinking, "This doesn't tell
me anything I don't already know. After
all, it's just a matter of common sense." If
this reflects your thoughts, I couldn't agree
with you more. But that's the point. You
do know all this. And it all amounts to
nothing more than the application of "horse
sense." Unfortunately, though we all possess an abundance of knowledge and sense,
the trick remains of how to get us to apply
this to the obvious situation. It has moved
some to muse that common sense is so un-

common that we seldom find it in use—and then only in the activity of those ordained great.

4. **Listen to Your Prospect.** Several messages are conveyed simultaneously in every sales call. Mr. Prospect's thoughts are conveyed through the meaning of his words. You will recall we referred to this earlier as his explicit message. That is, you are taking him at his word. Now, there is another message which is not expressed but nonetheless implied by his comments. Again, we have already called this his implicit message. Much to the dismay of most salesmen, it is not what Mr. Prospect says, but what he fails to say, that furnishes the bridge to understanding and, ultimately, to a successful conclusion and sale.

Know that your prospect's implied message expresses his real feelings or needs and wants of that particular moment. You must be listening, as a matter of fact, with your third ear to recognize these implications. You will be able to accomplish this aim by listening between the lines and dealing with Mr. Prospect's intentions. Cultivating the habit of continually analyzing his motives should prove especially useful. You might ask yourself: What does he mean besides what he is saying; how does he seem to feel today; what does he appear to really want; what does he actually need? Remember that while doing this, you must keep up your end of the conversation. With practice, it should almost come to be second nature to you. Incidentally, a natural benefit of this technique is that your prospect must participate a good deal in the dialogue. This makes it possible for you to listen with the third ear.

Skeptical? Perhaps you are thinking:

"Who actually needs these two channels of

conversation? Why doesn't he stand up like a man and say what's really on his mind?"

Don't blame him. If you must condemn something, censure society or civilization. Children, as you know, say what they think without any qualms whatsoever. It is only in growing up that one learns to adapt to the complex rules of customs and etiquette. Yet, despite this imposition and regimentation, human nature will not be still. It insists on a voice. As a result, a compromise is reached and this voice is expressed through implicit conversation. By implication you can praise and reassure yourself or insult, reject, and derogate others. Imagine how conveniently you can "air" your wants and thus avoid the possible embarrassment that would follow open discussion. Incidentally, humor is often used as a subtle attempt to convey a corrosive message without demeaning or damaging the reputation of the sender.

Listen to these prospects:

Mr. I: I put this place on its feet. Now, mister, that took work—backbreaking, hard work. But if I hadn't been willing or able to do it, who would, I ask you? . . .

MEANING: Give me credit; give me a personal buildup; or "see how clever I am." This could be a lack of self-confidence.

Mr. Attacker: Did you know Mr. Worm, the guy I replaced? He sure was a real wooden head, wasn't he? Why, the stories they tell on him! Let me tell you . . .

MEANING: Take a good look at me. I'm Mr. Big. By comparison everyone else is small. Remember that, Boy! This type of person seems to enjoy minimizing the exploits of others, no matter how worthwhile they may be. His negative inclination is graphically revealed in his incessant teasing and gossiping about the misfortunes or difficulties of others, including yourself. This man wears a shallow mask of words with which he shields his aggressive and hostile personality. Your natural temptation will be to meet him on his own terms. This should be discouraged. Often what he aspires to be catches the heat of his tongue. He would, therefore, not take kindly to your consensus attack. In this case, give him no cause to feel a challenge from you.

Mr. Demander: It sure must be nice being on the gravy train, expense account and all. I don't blame you, though. Might as well blow it as give it to Uncle Sam. Say, by the way, I've been meaning to ask you if you entertain a lot?

MEANING: Must be about time you asked my wife and I out to dinner, cheapskate. This is a blatant attempt to play on a salesman's desire to please. Of course, two can play this game. You may say, "No, I don't entertain a lot. Frankly, I don't want the customer to think I'm trying to buy his business. I want him to feel perfectly free to boot my fanny out if I'm not delivering. However, once I'm satisfied that he's satisfied, well, that's a different story . . ." He will get the point.

Mr. Controller: Were I in your shoes, son, I'd demand—that's right, demand the southern territory. Why, there i nothing around here. Like to help you, but you see, I'm what you call, "small potatoes."

MEANING: Can't you see you're wasting your time around here? I'm not about to buy from you. A prospect who handles you thusly indicates a need (dependence) for the esteem of others. He just doesn't have the heart to tell you to "beat it!"

5. **Give and Get Feedback of Your Prospect's Thinking.** You must check periodically for understanding. At intervals during the discussion, check for clarity by having your prospect feed back to you his interpretation of what you have said. In doing this, you will get an insight into his thinking. At the same time, the idiom of your ideas and the cadence of your thinking can be compared to his. What's more, you will learn how to influence him by feeding back an image which logically follows from what he has said. Carefully done, you can actually change his position. That is to say, your ideas may become "his" ideas. Then, you will not be selling him anything. He will simply be buying from you.

6. **Hold Your Prospect's Attention.** No doubt you have heard of the donkey that was in the middle of the road and wouldn't move. A motorist tried every conceivable way to cajole this beast into allowing him the right of way. Finally, a farmer wandered by and was apprised of the problem. Without delay, he approached the jackass, violently clubbed it over the head, and then gently led it to the side of the road. "You've got to get its attention first," remarked the farmer in a matter-of-fact manner.

Such a reminder is not necessarily the case for your Mr. Prospect, though sometimes you may be tempted to consider this seriously. Certainly, competition for his attention is ever present. Add to this the fact that we can concentrate well only on one thing at a time and you start to appreciate the problem. Knowing this, salesmen should avoid, whenever possible, conducting sales calls in waiting rooms or making sales presentations while in standing positions. In either case, it nullifies the salesman's effectiveness.

On the other hand, it is not enough to be comfortably situated and conveniently isolated with your prospect. Your listener's attention will still only be held if what you have to say is:

a. Useful.
b. Easy to grasp.
c. Worth the time it takes to tell it.
d. Economical in words and time.

What does this suggest to you? If you have decided it is planning, you are correct. It is only with a plan that you could ever hope to accomplish these four steps, each and every call. Planning, of course, is work. There will always be a temptation to avoid it for this explicit reason. But let us examine what it does for us. This should, if nothing else, give us pause to consider its value to us. For instance, it assists us in:

a. **Sticking to the Point**—which helps us to convey the ideas we want him to grasp.

b. **Avoiding Irrelevancies**—which keeps us from losing control or going astray, to the bewilderment and confusion of Mr. Prospect.

c. **Keeping Our Speeches Short**—which assists us in telling a simple and meaningful story. Incidentally, don't ever assume he knows (or wants to know) as much as you

115

do about your product, service, or program. This goes back to the problem of false assumption.

d. **Pacing Our Presentation to the Prospect's Speed of Comprehension**—which prevents us from being too slow and losing him, or too fast, with him shrugging his shoulders in an expression of futility or "why bother."

e. **Bringing in Fresh Information**—which gives us an opportunity to dramatize our ideas in a refreshing way. Think—what would really appeal to Mr. Prospect?

f. **Using Repetition**—which recrystallizes our ideas in a useful form. If he has missed the point, we can tune him in to our ideas without any embarrassment to him.

7. **Activate Prospect's Thinking.** Know that if your meaning is clear, your message will get into the mind of your prospect. You will recall an earlier reference to the three levels of hearing. Let us now consider them in a listening context. There is, then, the:

a. **Listening (Nonhearing Level).** Your prospect feigns attention but isn't really listening at all.

b. **Hearing (Nonthinking Level).** Your prospect hears the words but does not absorb the ideas.

c. **Thinking (Listening, Hearing, and Thinking Levels Merge into Comprehension).** Your prospect thinks about what you have said.

It should come as no surprise that your listener prefers to avoid thinking because this is work. The burden of stimulating his thinking, consequently, falls on you. Never an easy chore, it can nonetheless be accomplished by asking intelligent and relevant questions. A few such questions are mentioned below:

a. **Open Question.** This is a disarming type of query which makes your prospect feel important.

EXAMPLE: "Mr. Prospect, what do you think of our program (product or service)?"

b. **Reflective Question.** When you appear to be losing his interest and attention, this might be employed.

EXAMPLE: "Mr. Prospect, you seem to be concerned about the initial costs involved or you appear to have some doubts about this program?" This should invigorate his thinking and continue his responsiveness, not to mention reassure him that you have his best interests at heart.

c. **Directed Question.** Perchance you have noted during the course of the call a special interest in a feature or benefit of what you're selling. This type question can then be used.

EXAMPLE: "Mr. Prospect, earlier you indicated a liking for the convenient form of our product. Would you mind explaining to me exactly how this would benefit you?" His comment will, then, enlarge the area of your common agreement.

d. **Restatement Question.** Once you are well into your presentation, it is wise to check for understanding.

EXAMPLE: "Mr. Prospect, this program will in no way disrupt your present operation. Would you like me to enlarge on this point?"

e. **Summarizing Question.** In order to be certain of understanding, it might be well to use this.

EXAMPLE: "Mr. Prospect, have we covered all parts of the program to your satisfaction?" If you haven't, he will surely let you know.

f. **Justifying Question.** Caution and tact must be used when you wish to shake your prospect out of his obstinacy or, possibly, his lethargy. You may accomplish this by opening up his thinking.

EXAMPLE: "Mr. Prospect, can you be sure your equipment is clean? What evidence do you have that no problem exists?"

g. **Hypothetical Question.** This, too, opens up his mind. In this case, it involves planting a new idea.

EXAMPLE: "Mr. Prospect, did you see where Merton-Fox started this program? Since they've been on stream with this, production costs have dropped 20%. Do you think it is a fair assumption to make that a similar system, such as yours, would do as well, if not better?"

h. **Exploratory Question.** This might be used to find out details relating to the nature and complexity of his problem.

EXAMPLE: "Mr. Prospect, would you mind explaining how you happened to discover this problem? What exactly did you find?"

118

i. Leading Question. This may be employed as a method of planting an idea or of leading your prospect to a greater understanding.

EXAMPLE: "Mr. Prospect, what are you now doing? How long have you been doing this? Who is responsible for controlling this? Why do you think you will need service? How much service do you consider adequate?" The leading type question is an important means of canvassing. Used effectively, it saves time and gets to the heart of a problem in a precise manner. When considering this technique, it is well to recall the practical words of Rudyard Kipling:

> I keep six honest serving men,
> They taught me all I knew.
> Their names are *what* and *why* and
> *when* and *how* and *where* and *who*.

Probing a prospect's mind with questions is a gentle and kind, as well as profitable journey, in the hands of a truly professional salesman. Admittedly, it takes time, patience, and persistence to develop this excellent sales tool. And even then, there is still the danger or temptation to get "cute" with this power —for make no mistake, it is a form of power. What you are doing is pointing another person's mind in a particular direction and then asking him to find the solution you have already picked out for him. As you acquire this skill, therefore, employ it with increasing respect, if not reverence.

8. **Deal with Prospect Resistance.** Persuading someone to accept your way of thinking makes it necessary that he surrender his former position. This means that he must inevitably pass through a stage of re-

sistance. He may listen to you, comprehend the very essence of your program, and even do what you ask of him—for the moment. After his euphoric feeling passes, his spirit of generosity, you may discover that he has not accepted your thinking at all. On the contrary, you realize that he is not sold on anything you have said. Until your prospect disassociates himself from his former way of operating (and thinking), an order means very little inasmuch as it represents neither a new account nor a customer. This, next to closing, is the most critical, if not the most difficult step of selling. Indeed, here we find what a salesman is made of. For example, Mr. Prospect may have given you a good order. But you find on a subsequent visit that he is not using your material. Or you find he is still following the old procedures of competition, even though he has contracted your program or service. You have a problem. How you handle it will determine the future of this account. In a word, it shall test your mettle.

Next to acquiring new business, nothing is more important than the holding of it once acquired.

There are, to be sure, many ways of looking at this problem. You may, for instance, after having lost an account, turn your back on it—thereby admitting defeat. The game for you is truly over because you have lost your fight. Or you may see through the whole situation and recognize it for the temporary setback that it is. In this sense it stirs your professional pride, spurring you on to reclaim what you believe to be rightly yours. Conversely, should it be you who has won the account, the selling situation has a different aspect. Yet, it too may present some knotty problems. It all depends on you. Were you to savor your triumph by sitting on your hands, chances are you would become vulnerable almost immediately. But should you set to work with enthusiasm, diligence, and purpose, stability would certainly emerge from your initial success. How you handle the normal contingencies of selling, then, will determine the nature of the final outcome. Will you win the battles but lose the wars? Or will you use the battles to win the wars? What shall it be?

Meeting Resistance Effectively

Implied in all this are the following words of caution:

Be always suspect of too easy a sale.

Before you congratulate yourself on a job well done, press your new customer for a commitment to action, remaining unsatisfied until this is realized. That is, continue the intensity of your sales effort until there is concrete evidence that he has indeed accepted change. Otherwise, most assuredly competition will wrest the account from you or your program will fail from lack of care. In either case, you lose.

When you encounter opposition or resistance, you must evaluate its rational and irrational elements in order to know precisely how to deal with it. If it is largely rational, it is only a matter of weighing the facts. Your selling problem is clear cut. All you have to do is arrive at distinct advantages to your program or service and obvious disadvantages to your prospect's present operation. He will do the rest.

Now, if his resistance is primarily irrational, weighing the facts very carefully will not work because he is not guided by them. Incidentally, this is where many salesmen reach a frustrating impasse with their clients. They insist on treating each man as a reasonable and rational person—no doubt after themselves—despite the evidence to the contrary. Technical salesmen are especially guilty of this faux pas. Mr. Prospect, when he is resisting you on primarily irrational grounds, opposes you for reasons he wishes to conceal from you or even himself. Of course, it could be that he is simply afraid to change. Another possibility is he may resent having others trying to influence him. And don't overlook the chance that he may personally dislike you. So complex is this opposition that it is never easy to discern, let alone define. But you would be more than remiss if you neglected its proper scrutiny, nonetheless. For you can be certain of one thing, this opposition will not fade away by ignoring it.

See if you recognize anyone from these common irrational characteristics found in some problem personalities:

1. **Vehemence.** When the opposition to your program, service, product, or idea is unnaturally violent, you may be sure that Mr. Prospect has an already surfeited bag of troubles. Obviously, he is not comfortable in his position and he may see you as a further threat to his security.

2. **Unresponsive Attitude.** Clinging to a fixed position of resistance without considering a counter-suggestion, denotes the serving of a private need. He may have a stereotype picture in his mind of what a salesman is. Then, no matter how valuable you may actually be to him, it is nigh impossible to penetrate his wooden view.

3. **Rationalizing.** Trying to make it seem logical to hold a contrary position when it isn't reasonable is an attempt at concealment. I have made engineering surveys of production systems which clearly indicated that savings up to 50% could be realized by imple-

menting a sound program. Yet, an engineer, while agreeing in principle with me, would argue that he wouldn't want to commence such a program until his system was cleaned up. In other words, he would want the program after the fact or when it was no longer needed. Logic appeals little to such a man. Still, he wants a salesman's approval—but for unknown private reasons—certainly not his program.

4. **Objection Hopping.** Before you are able to answer his objection, he gives you another, and then another, and then still another. What he is doing is hiding behind a wall of excuses.

What do you do about these difficult people? Do you ignore them? Do you meet resistance with resistance? Do you get "cute" with them? Of course, you do none of these. As a professional salesman you find ways of assisting them in helping themselves. You excavate their buried positive personalities. Here are some ways you might begin:

   a. **Express Understanding.** Show kindness and genuine interest in the prospect and his position. Give him the support that may be missing in his job. And by all means, be patient and don't debate.

   b. **Make the Prospect Aware That He Is Resisting.** You may say, "You don't seem very willing to discuss this program with me. I'm wondering if there is something my company or I have done to annoy you."

   c. **Evaluate the Prospect's Objections with Him.** "Could you tell me more about why changeover concerns you so much?", or "What specifically don't you like about this system?", or "Would you mind enlarging on your reservations about the time, control, and cost of our program?"

123

    d. **Believe in Him and He Will Believe in Himself.**

    e. **Trust Him and He Will Trust You.**

Before you consider these suggestions academic and dismiss them, try them on your difficult prospects. Remember, there is this solace for us all: If he has proven difficult for you, it is more than likely that others have found him the same. Your advantage over your colleagues, however, is a great deal more than a commonly shared difficulty. It is the knowledge gleaned from probing into why he behaves as he does and an acceptance of the man as you find him. This drop of kindness and understanding from you may very well bring a flood of gratitude from him.

How to Sell the Tough Customers

Although it would be unwise to categorize prospects into types, there are enough general characteristics commonly encountered in many of them to at least justify these pseudosurnames:

Mr. Silent

Mr. Procrastinator

Mr. Glad-Hander

Mr. Methodical

Mr. Overcautious

Mr. Opinionated

Mr. Skeptical

Mr. Grouch

Mr. Argumentative

The irrational overtones that can become so confounding to a salesman can be dealt with on a systematic basis. As a matter of fact, that is about the only way they can be successfully negotiated.

Let us now examine these perplexing "gentlemen" and consider practical tactics which might be employed to penetrate their emotional screen and win them over:

Mr. Silent. Communicating with him is difficult because he is nearly totally passive. He is reluctant to discuss his situation or even the point the salesman is making. It is especially hard to get a commitment out of him. But why is he silent? Actually, you may never know. It could be one or a combination of several reasons. Perhaps he doesn't know how to converse. He may be a deep thinker or merely a fatuous person. Then again, it could be that he lacks confidence which has resulted in his being unusually cautious.

> **Stratagem:** Question him, using types requiring his opinion or asking him to amplify on various points made in your presentation. Don't ask questions that would expose his ignorance or prove in any way embarrassing to him. Make them of such a personal nature that he feels comfortable answering them. Visual aids as sales tools can also be helpful in obtaining participation from him. Ask him questions about them. A salesman should exercise real patience in waiting for his reply. Sometimes silence is golden. This is such a time. When you pause or ask a question, you should expect a response. Don't make a verbal rush to fill the void. Should no response be forthcoming, look expectantly at the prospect, encouraging him to answer. Find out what really interests him. It may be necessary to talk about such topics until he is reassured and receptive, even though they may be totally irrelevant to your reason for making the call.

Mr. Procrastinator. Many people find it difficult to make a decision. But Mr. P is more than an undecided person; he is a veritable bundle of nervous energy, programmed to standard replies at the very mention of change. Decision time for him is always tomorrow. Listen to him:

* "Let me think it over. I'll get back to you in a few days."
* "Tell you what, I'll bring it up at our meeting next week."
* "I'll talk it over with my people and let you know."
* "I'm still evaluating your proposal. Won't be long now."
* "I've got your card. I'll call you in a couple of days. Okay?"

Do these replies sound familiar? Procrastinators have more "one liners" or excuses for postponing a decision than any other prospect you are likely to meet. They are constantly looking at "other alternatives" before deciding. It is as difficult for them to pick out a tie in the morning as it is to decide on a $10,000 proposition.

> Stratagem: You must be positive, self-assured, absolutely certain of your facts, and dramatic— but not overpoweringly so. Address him in a way that suggests you have confidence in his ability to make a decision. Showmanship is important as well. Summarize sales points several times. Repetition, a colorful presentation, and an aura of optimism will incline Mr. P towards your sales objectives. Yet, a receptive mood is not enough. You must close sharply and crisply, usually with an assumptive close, and then vanish!

Mr. Glad-Hander. Selling roles get mixed up here. I once had a salesman tell me a prospect was our greatest booster in the territory. He apparently knew several of our executives and was high on the worth of our whole company. Yet, he had never made the first purchase from us. A master salesman, he was saying "no" and making us like it. This is not an unusual feat for Mr. Glad-Hander. He appears to like salesmen and they seem to reciprocate by letting him sell them. This type of individual frequently agrees with much of what you have to say—even complimenting you on your presentation or carefully worded proposal. He may even go so far as to say that you are the only salesman he wants to deal with. But put sales pressure on him to act and he changes colors. Either he becomes indignant or irrelevant. Never forget:

> Someone is sold in every sales situation. Either you sell him on his need for you or he sells you on his satisfaction with what he has and is doing.

Mr. Glad-Hander is a consummate artist in recognizing and then exploiting this distinction.

> **Stratagem:** Control of the interview is difficult with this individual. You must be alert to his attempts to throw you off course. By all means ignore his flattering irrelevancies. Bring him back to the sales presentation or situation by saying, "By the way, that reminds me . . ." In this manner, you maintain control and keep him on track. Be brief and summarize key points in cogent terms. Don't attempt to match his nervous energy or enthusiasm. Instead, feed him ideas and materials with which your program can be related. Chances are he is a moving target for very good reasons. For instance, a crippling flaw in his personality may be at the root of his "glad-handing." This flaw may be anything from alcoholism to pure incompetence. In any case, you must work to show him that you are on his side, and that

you will relieve—not add to—his burdens. Be all business, no nonsense, and concentrate on what you are there to do. Fight the temptation to play the nice guy—the role, incidentally, he would have you play.

Mr. Methodical. Many times the salesman overlooks this individual, believing a slow reaction indicates a lack of interest or a lack of ability to think and communicate. You are apt to be too rapid for him even when you recognize him as a real prospect. That is, you make the false assumption that since he is methodical he communicates easily and thinks quickly. Remember this:

> There is no relationship between a person being methodical and having the ability to communicate and think.

He may, for example, be methodical because he has a strong need for autonomy or self-rule, which means he will likely resist influence or coercion. He may have a strong need for order, meaning that he may arrange or organize everything with scrupulous precision. Or he may have a strong need for knowledge to satisfy an inquiring mind bent on exploring, looking, listening, and inspecting. In other words, Mr. M may have a brilliant or chaotic mind. He cannot be taken for granted under any circumstances. That is certain.

> **Stratagem:** You must slow down and accept the prospect's speed of thought and verbal transmission. Preparation for a call on this individual should involve particular attention to details and specifics relating to your subject. When asking a question, you should wait patiently for a reply. Mind you, this man may be juggling a number of variables before he answers. So it is wise for

you to let him set the pace. Listening is a vital technique in this instance.

Mr. Overcautious. Overwhelmed by much that surrounds him, unsure and suspect of many of his own thoughts, he continuously seeks advice from others. What's more, his confidant may be a casual acquaintance or an intimate friend. He is neither discrete nor distinct in such matters. Consequently, a subordinate or a wife may hold an inordinate control over him. At the same time, his sense of insecurity and dependence is displayed by a strong need for friendship or associations. Even cooperating and conversing with others socially is hardly done on a casual basis, as it, too, involves the fulfillment of a need. Mr. Overcautious may reveal himself in other ways as well. For instance, he may indicate a strong desire for reassurance, protection, and sympathy. Usually, he admires and willingly follows his superior. And he is known to cooperate in the same spirit with outside advisers, such as professional salesmen, gladly. This could and does stem from a combination of negative drives: fear of failure, shame, humiliation, ridicule, or embarrassment. Whatever the force controlling him, any attempt to move him from what he knows will be met with resistance. In other words, the salesman who would seem to have it made is the one who has the business now.

> **Stratagem:** Concentrate on evidence and facts which are easily verified. These are the visual materials your organization provides. Here is a partial listing:
>
> National Advertising Summaries
> *Sales Portfolios*
> Annual Reports
> *Testimonials*

129

Sales and Service Literature
List of Satisfied Accounts

This is used in an attempt to build the confidence of this timid person. You should assemble the facts on hand in such a way as to justify his making a decision to buy. Relate your program to his emotional needs. Then, communicate to him, by either word or action, that you believe he has the ability and the courage to decide—to make a decision. There is a very different approach which you may be overlooking. Perhaps it is so obvious that you have discounted its efficacy. Consider the prospect and think what you could bring him beyond a product, service, or idea. Might it be a poised, calm, and reassuring influence? Might it be you? Your ability and willingness to listen with understanding is in short supply. No one knows this better than Mr. Overcautious. Now, think what effect this would have on him. Most likely, it would fill an emotional void. Remember this:

> All of us are emotional animals. When we are distressed, we seek comfort and solace, often in others. Sometimes, like an oasis in the desert, a person is seen as a wellspring to fulfillment, if not survival. Quite frequently, the person seen as most able to satisfy this need is the salesman.

Small wonder that the friendship between a salesman and his customers is such a cherished relationship.

Mr. Opinionated. This person apparently knows all the answers. He knows all about your company, your products and services, even your industry. In fact, he knows all about anything you have to say before you have had an opportunity to present the facts. From the moment you introduce yourself, he will most assuredly wrest control of the interview. He thinks his own judgment, opinions, and hunches are nigh infallible and he will react negatively to the slightest innuendo or suggestion to the contrary. Loaded questions and irrelevant technical considerations are apt to be used if his will is not accepted. It is quite understandable why many salesmen abhor the thought of calling on him. This gives us good cause to wonder about the man behind the mask. To wit, what is below the surface of this man's facade? Everyone has a need for a sense of achievement. It only differs in degree. With Mr. Opinionated we find this need runs quite high. That is, whereas, we all have a need to overcome some obstacles, to exercise some influence, and to accomplish something distinctly our own, this grows into an obsession with him. Such an ego-involved person finds his needs increase in magnitude and immediacy. Never satiated, Mr. Opinionated strives for recognition and prompt action.

Examine his disposition:

> He has a self-forwarding attitude and a tendency to seek praise and commendation; to demand respect, to crave distinction; to attract attention; to excite, shock, or amuse; to dominate, control, or influence; to persuade, dictate, direct, or restrain; or to organize the lives and conduct of others.

> Stratagem: The golden rule in this case is to make him feel important. This is evidently what he needs and so you cater to it. Keep this in mind always:

> > Never project your ideas in a conclusive context, but seek his advice, counsel, and opinion.

This means that you will control the interview by accepting him as he is and by using this knowledge in a constructive fashion. Your facts and ideas become his facts and ideas; your objectives become his objectives. A purposeful but permissive format guides you through his obstacle course. In fact, your entire attitude is permissive. To challenge him would no doubt create a conflict, perhaps a conflict in personalities. This would be most imprudent from a selling standpoint. Give him the day, the hour, and the minute. And he will give you the order.

Mr. Skeptical. Listen to him. He has a negative answer for virtually everything. Moreover, he knows the when, why, and where about everything you discuss. He may feel, for example, very strongly about specific points—such as cost, quality, delivery, control, etc. You can be certain that he will labor assiduously at them. In addition, he is difficult to work with inasmuch as it is nearly impossible to communicate with him. Why such an attitude? As usual, there is no one answer to his disposition. It is just possible, however, that this person has a need to dominate, to receive recognition, or to feel superior. He may even have a strong need to snub, ignore, or exclude others—to remain aloof and indifferent. On the other hand, it may be a screen or defense mechanism. Possibly, he senses the need to justify his actions or to resist probing for fear of disclosure. And, of course, no one is more suspect to him than a salesman—a person whom he considers a legal liar.

Stratagem: Emphasize the facts. Use logic and syllogistic reasoning. That is, tie reasonable premises together with proper conclusions. Beware of false reasoning, such as this:

Cows have four legs.
Horses have four legs.
Therefore, cows are horses.

Absurd you say! This is exactly how it sounds to this prospect when you are not careful of your facts or the use of your reasoning power. What's more, hide nothing from him. No product is perfect. No program is foolproof. Volunteer such information when it is apropos. Otherwise, he may discover it himself and use it against you. But even though this person has a tendency to argue and be steadfast in his opinion, he will yield to logic when properly presented.

Mr. Grouch. Never start the interview with the inane question:

How are things going?

If you have ever done this, you know exactly what I mean. What inevitably follows is a tirade about his health, job, friends, business, state of the world, etc. Mr. Grouch is always ready to complain—always ready to relate rumors and opinions which would denigrate others. His outlook is totally pessimistic and, predictably, he finds most conditions intolerable. The future holds no promise or hope. But study his face. Don't be surprised to see that he derives some pleasure from his storehouse of morbid misgivings.

Stratagem: As difficult as it may be, hear this man out. You might also display patience and maintain your natural buoyancy. Be optimistic and give him constructive ideas. And above all, don't absorb his pessimism. This is, indeed, a time when a strong offense is the best defense. That is to say, cheer him up and bring him out of his doldrums. Demonstrate your action program. Show him how your product or service will solve his problem. Attack him with enthusiasm and you will leave him smiling, if not laughing.

Mr. Argumentative. He wants to argue, to take issue

with anything that is said. He is a provocateur. A nemesis to the salesman, especially the beginner, he delights in making demanding and sarcastic remarks to "cut the salesman down to size." His pet names reflect his disposition. To him a salesman is among other things:

> A 'peddler' fleecing the public for 'that outfit' with a product that is 'pure poppycock' and a service which is a 'license to steal.'

These expressions hardly endear him to the hard-working professional salesman. But he accepts them philosophically, nonetheless, and smiles in the face of them. He knows that Mr. A would like nothing better than to get his dander up. He would argue with anyone simply for the sake of arguing. Quite insincere, Mr. Argumentative enjoys trying his victim's patience. Why? Despite all the evidence to the contrary, he is basically an insecure individual. This may express itself in a need to dominate, influence, or control others. Or it may be shown in a need to belittle, harm, slander, blame, accuse, or maliciously ridicule a person. Or it may even indicate a need for power over things, people, and ideas—things outside the self.

> **Stratagem:** Don't argue with him. Be purposeful, firm, and stand your ground, but be patient and understanding as well. Even though this is extremely difficult, consider how few probably have made an attempt to know him. By doing this you give him the recognition he so badly craves. Then too, being philosophical with a touch of humor helps, as this illustrates below:
>
>> A salesman became ill and it was necessary for his manager to keep an important appointment with the bellicose Mr. A. Surprised at seeing the salesman's manager, he thun-

dered, 'What are you doing here? I
expected Phil.' The manager replied
with a knowing smile, 'Didn't you
know? It's my day to be in the cage.'
So unexpected was this rejoinder
that Mr. A practically collapsed in
laughter. He saw the inference very
clearly. As a result, the tension was
broken and new respect won.

Do you understand why?

This has been a very long discussion, covering what I
believe to be the most crippling phase of selling—the selling
impasse. Worry and anxiety build up to paralyzing pro-
portions when this is reached. It logically follows, then, that
if you penetrate this obstacle, you are free to let the worry
out and put the joy back in the profession of selling.

So, if at this point you see Mr. Smith (see page 87)
as a difficult but not impossible "dead head"—if you see
him as a challenge, not a hopeless cause—then, you have
gotten somewhere. Use this material as a reference and as
a source of help when you are in trouble with Mr. Prospect.
Several concepts have been discussed. The essential one,
though, is the *why* of prospect behavior. And explicit in
this text are many methods of handling all types of people
in all kinds of situations. Now, I ask you. Who is to be sold?

SELF-STUDY QUESTIONS:

Let us consider the case history of Mr. Young.

Mr. Young directs a departmental staff of three research engineers and two technical secretaries. He occupies a separate office from the rest of his staff.

Looking somewhat like a fashion ad from *Playboy Magazine*, his lithe athletic 6-foot frame is accentuated by a casual grace and poise. Yet, incongruous with this is his practiced smile which threatens at any moment to tighten into a smirk. His eyes, alert and combatant, further betray the composure of his person. He is 34 years old.

Everything about his office is unpretentious and functional, a true reflection of the plant environment. No pictures or certificates, save a peculiar calendar and map of the 15th Century, adorn the walls. A small glass-covered bookcase houses his library of engineering and technical books and trade journals. Some 30 titles on metallurgy, metallurgical chemistry, and chemical engineering give a clue to his job function, if not his deep passion for knowledge, for these books appear worn and well-used. No dust collects here. His desk is a disarray of journals, papers, diagrams, and general minutiae. You get the impression that this is more than a work area; it is a den of pleasure. But strangely enough, what sets it apart is the striking incongruity of a freshly cut yellow rose embellishing the credenza.

You are greeted with a friendly, rather casual handshake and a crisp, "Good morning!" His attention from the first is keen; his gaze, steady, even piercing, as you make your way through your presentation. His comments, when proffered, are to the point; his queries, likewise, are incisive. Each is made in a smooth, level tone with but a trace of aplomb.

Any technical consideration in your presentation will

elicit a careful response, clearly indicating comprehension and technical rapport. Sometimes, unfortunately, he slips into condescension.

Interruptions are handled without a break in his composure. Be it a phone call, or the appearance of a subordinate, the situation is always well under control. He takes pains to make his work seem effortless. Other aspects of his personality are revealed when he is away from the plant. For instance, his conversational tone has a lilt found missing at the plant—more natural, more alive. The mention of travel, luxurious living, the "Club," or the pleasures of sailing swings him into this becoming orbit. Only his most recent bridge finesse can successfully compete with this. Occasionally, on the other hand, he waxes serious and comments on current events, never on politics, per se. It is safe to say, nevertheless, that he reflects the politics of his time.

When he makes up his mind, as he did in this case, he calls a meeting with the general manager and plant superintendent. They are briefed on your proposal and then comments are solicited. The consensus is usually in support of Mr. Young's recommendations.

Discussion of Mr. Young's case history:

1. What kind of a man is Mr. Young?
2. What do you think would appeal to him?
3. What might antagonize him?
4. Do you think Mr. Young would be difficult to sell? Why?
5. Let us consider how we might get through to him. From what you have seen, heard, and uncovered, what would you say are Mr. Young's three most dominant emotional needs or desires?

    a. Ego-building
    b. Ambition

    c. Security

    d. Self-approval

    e. Social approval

    f. Power-domination

    g. Conservatism

6. What benefits would appeal to him? Why?

7. How do you plan to use this information to close?

RECOMMENDED FURTHER READING:

Heinz L. Ansbacher, Ph.D. and Rowena R. Ansbacher, Ph.D. *The Individual Psychology of Alfred Adler* (Basic Books, Inc., 1956).

James Bender. *How to Talk Well* (McGraw-Hill Book Company, Inc., 1949).

Alexis Carrel, M.D. *Man, the Unknown* (Harper & Brothers Publishers, 1935).

N. C. Christensen. *The Art of Persuasion in Selling* (Parker Publishing Company, Inc., 1970).

Glenn Clark. *A Man's Reach* (Harper & Brothers Publishers, 1949).

Glenn J. Cook. *The Art of Making People Listen to You* (Parker Publishing Co., Inc., 1967).

Thomas Dreier. *We Human Chemicals* (The Updegraff Press, Ltd., 1948).

Rudolf Flesch, Ph.D. *How to Make Sense* (Gramercy Publishing Company, 1954).

Les Giblin. *How to Have Confidence and Power in Dealing with People* (Prentice-Hall, Inc., 1956).

Albert Goldstein. *Secrets of Overcoming Sales Resistance: 386 Tested Replies to Objections* (Parker Publishing Company, Inc., 1969).

S. I. Hayakawa, Ph.D. *Language in Action* (Harcourt, Brace & World, Inc., 1939).

Napoleon Hill. *Think and Grow Rich* (The Ralston Society, 1942).

A. A. Luce, M.C., D.D., Litt.D. *Logic* (The English Universities Press, Ltd., 1958).

Maxwell Maltz, M.D., F.I.C.S. *Psycho-Cybernetics* (Prentice-Hall, Inc., 1960).

Karl A. Menninger, M.D. *The Human Mind* (Alfred A. Knopf, 1964).

Andre Missenard. *In Search of Man* (Hawthorn Books, Inc., 1957).

Jesse S. Nirenberg, Ph.D. *Getting Through to People* (Prentice-Hall, Inc., 1968).

Russel Conwell Ross. *Speak with Ease* (Funk & Wagnalls Company, 1961).

Bertrand Russell. *Education of Character* (Philosophical Library, Inc., 1961).

James R. Simmons. *The Quest for Ethics* (Philosophical Library, Inc., 1962).

Everett B. Wilson, and Sylvia B. Wright. *Getting Along with People in Business* (Funk & Wagnalls Company, 1950).

(5) Reasons for Succeeding—The Power of Dynamic Motivation

Sit back and relax. Make yourself comfortable. Comfortable? Fine. Now, ask yourself this question:

"What is it I really want out of life?"

Have you thought of this lately? Chances are you haven't. I wonder why. Don't you find it a little strange that seldom, if ever, we think about where we are and where we are going? No question about it, most people drift through life, merely existing. But herein lies an important paradox. Much as we would seem not to care, apparently there is an unconscious struggle within us to level with ourselves—to quit pretending that we don't care when we know full well we care very much. It has been said that there is a burning desire within us all to get on with life and to become one

140

with our destiny. Frustration, anxiety, and depression—
what are they but reminders that we are not listening to
our real desires and not moving with providence.

Most of us, I'm afraid, wander through life with little
sense of direction or purpose. If you feel this statement
does not apply to you, consider yourself in exclusive company. Forgive me for finding this hard to believe. You see,
I know the people who find it difficult to fasten on to something and ride it through. Not until I began to write did I
know my direction or purpose with any degree of certainty.
Like you, I haunted the bookstores—always attempting to
find the answers "out there" somewhere. Well, I'm afraid
it's not out there, but somewhere inside—"inside you." So,
as I remonstrated to you in the beginning, the monkey is
indeed on your back. I discovered mine and I hope to help
you discover and master yours.

Now, both of us are salesmen. How a man wanders
into this profession, consequently, has a common significance because it affects us all collectively. That is to say,
just as we are salesmen as individuals, we have, at the same
time, a collective identity. No attempt will be made here
to precisely define that identity. Suffice it to say that
selling seems a melting pot or mix batch of mostly capable
people—an accidental profession, as it were, which finds
the individual salesman recreating his job function to in-
flect his frustrated ambitions. For instance, the frustrated
teacher turned salesman would use his "pedantic muscle"
to persuade clients to buy; the would-be scientist finds himself ever searching for the problem situation; the artist
turned "mercenary" continuously attempts to elevate the
profession to the cultural climate he seeks; the frustrated
medic practices his "bedside manner" with each and every
prospect in physical or mental turmoil; and the frustrated

"man of the cloth" manifests his crusading zeal in community affairs, if not on the job. Only the salesman, in it strictly for the money, is untouched by these psychic overtones. But he appears to be a vanishing breed. Money, in itself, is not sufficient compensation to motivate the modern salesman. Lest this be mistaken, he indeed has a money drive. But more important, he has a need to be of value—to be of service and worth to others. Unfortunately, what he is and what he wants to be is not very clear to him. Too little time has been spent on this crucial factor. He may have drive and desire, but without direction motivation becomes a desultory force—a power consuming its source, the salesman, rather than launching and sustaining him on a career ship. The fact that total failure seldom occurs does not mitigate the problem. Nor does the fact that worry and frustration, tending to strangle and distort a person's unique motivation or reasons for succeeding, justify our apprehension or insulation. On the contrary, they should knock us out of our lethargy. But I should talk! For I, after all, have bounded like a tennis ball in quest of my motivation.

Like most other salesmen, selling proved a fortuitous rather than a planned vocation. Albeit trained as a chemist, I soon became disenchanted with chemical bench work. My first thought, upon realizing this, was to acquire a graduate degree in chemistry and teach. This desire was somewhat complicated by the fact that I had a wife and two small children to support. Not even a graduate fellowship, which I was awarded, with a two-year $4,000 stipend was sufficient to carry this load. It was quite apparent that I needed a job paying much more than I was then making to realize this ambition. The idea of selling popped into my head. Shortly thereafter, I found myself selling and servicing industrial water treatment chemicals. Drive, desire, and direction were working in consort for me. And not surprising, because of this harmony, I soon leaped to the lead over the less motivated more veteran salesmen. Even so, my career objective lay outside selling. In fact, plans had already been carefully formulated for leaving this successful venture for the academic clime. But that is as far as it ever went. It turned out that my wife had a surprise for me—number three was on the way. Close as we were cutting it, we knew this put an end to our academic dreams. Understandably, a period of transition followed. Drive and desire remained intact, but somehow direction had vanished like the wind. At this critical moment, pride stepped in and took over. I had been the leading salesman too long to surrender the hill without a fight. Still, even a warrior tires of the battle, I was to discover, though he be the victor. Then, the idea of money—of accumulating the green stuff —came to intrigue me. This, too, sustained me until I was well into the double figures and began to accumulate this green badge of success. Now, what to do? Panic commenced to set in. I looked about to see if anyone noticed me. No one had. They were too busy fumbling along like me. I looked for the answers in books; they were not there. I looked in the eyes of other salesmen and thought I saw a hint of the answer. I took courage in this. My thoughts, ideas, misgivings, hopes, and doubts were winning their ears. Salesmen were asking me questions. What's more, they were listening to my replies. Management and training responsibilities fell to me. I found myself selling as I had never sold before, but it was no longer a product. It was the kinetic energy of creative ideas. The more I gave of myself, the more enriched I became. I discovered that the real learner in a teacher-pupil relationship is the teacher. There was so much to learn—so many to teach. My new motivation, not to mention love, was getting in the way of my executive duties. A choice had to be made. In my case, it meant that I must leave security and the known for greater enlightenment and opportunity to share my discovered secrets—secrets hidden within us all, secrets which show us the path to growth and fulfillment. So, at 36, I retired to write and think about my profession and how I might best serve it. This, my second book, is a product of this fruition and gestation. In a word, then, I have taken a most circuitous route in order to stumble into a slot that fit. How much more fortunate, if not less traumatic, it might have been. I hope in this telling I will help you avoid such a waste of this precious commodity—namely, you.

What Is Motivation?

Should you feel yourself outside such an experience or should you remain unconvinced that anything compares with one's money drive, now is your chance to see for sure. Let your mind open up so that it may accept and sort what is to follow. For it is equally important to us all to know what makes Sammy run. It could very well be that this modern protagonist is alter ego to many of us, if not all.

Motivation is admittedly a very complex subject. But you owe it to yourself, nevertheless, to isolate and explore this essential aspect of your human nature. It holds the key to the effective utilization of your inherent ability.

Let us define motivation as the inner urge that moves or prompts us to do something—to act in some way. Now, just imagine being able to put this precious thing under the microscope. As we adjust the fine lens of our scope, we note that motivation involves behavior—behavior which is stimulated, governed, and controlled by a set of singular traits and sentiments. Once in focus, we also see how this makes each of us unique as individuals. No two people can be seen possessing the same motivation. In fact, much as we would have "so and so" like "so and so," we observe that this is not possible. No one is really like anyone; that is, anyone save themselves. Scanning the microscopic field we realize that, like snowflakes against a common background, our uniqueness gets lost in accepting "similar to" as meaning "the same as." A large measure of our motivational difficulty lies within the bounds of this confusion. Nothing is more irrelevant in this life than that which motivates another person.

If only each of us would envy less and listen more carefully to our inner calling, motivation would truly burst through that wall of frustration and anxiety, if not loneliness and despair, to the high ground of peace and fulfillment. If only each of us would maintain our focus on ourselves and move according to our inner urging, motivation would indeed propel us to where we dream of going. No one understood this better or was able to capture this essence more clearly than Henry David Thoreau:

> If a man does not keep pace with his companions,
> perhaps it is because he hears a different drummer.
> Let him step to the music which he hears, however measured or far away.

If only each of us would sink his teeth into the meaning of this mental morsel, motivation would prevent our pace from slackening or the seeds of self-doubt from flourishing, choking off our creative energies. Yes, if only . . .

Motivation is more important than innate ability. I say this without qualification for two reasons. First, I have never been convinced that ability has been successfully perceived, measured, or evaluated. The propinquity of eclectic aptitudes in one person is analogous to identifying the parts to an engine. It fails to determine the horsepower. But if it could even achieve a calibration of this, there would remain the question of how much horsepower would actually be used. A truly motivated person uses as much horsepower as he can lay his hands upon. Second, motivation is the near perfect marriage of mentality with emotion. The two synergize to transcend the limitations other men would place upon the motivated man.

Think about this. If men of great motivation were to be moved more by their critics than their credos, we would just be discovering the wheel. Ironically, motivation—as it takes hold of a man—finds the scoffers becoming the sycophants. Our environs are fickle and transitory this way. Bill Lear of Lear Jets never saw a university, yet he is one of the most imaginative, creative engineering geniuses of our time. He has over 200 university-trained scientists and engineers in his employ. Many times over a millionaire, asked what he lived for doing, he replied, "Tackling an impossible project. I'm working on one right now, an automotive steam engine . . ." Surely, it is this quest for greater challenges, not money, that motivates Bill Lear to grow and grow. Somewhere along the line, he undoubtedly had to suffer people reminding him of his "educational handicap" or the sheer folly of his ambitions. Were he to have listened to these detractors, at this very moment the forces of frustration and anxiety, not to mention despair and desperation, could find him a broken man.

Each man has many reasons for succeeding floating around in the labyrinth of his mind. These reasons, nonetheless, remain an enigma to many of us. Too often we seek what we neither want nor need because other people

146

or things would cause us to so strive. Take the money drive, for instance. More than likely it is a cover for a deeper desire. Perhaps it is a cover for a secret desire to be more socially prominent—to be accepted socially by a more privileged class. Disillusionment is bound to follow if money, once acquired, does not win this acceptance. On the other hand, should money be the price of admission, there is the question of values, interests, and cultural experience which may drive an invisible wedge between you and the object of your striving. This is essentially what happened to the late F. Scott Fitzgerald, author of the *Lost Generation Period of American Literature*. He believed money would solve all his problems, emotional and otherwise. When it didn't and when he discovered that the super-rich differ little in character from the poor, he was stunned, never to recover. He died broken in spirit. To avoid such a possibility, it is important that we understand what we want and why we seek it.

How to Understand Motivation

To understand motivation it is necessary that you first be aware of the phenomenon of motivation. Know that it is not necessarily good or a positive force. Know, too, that it is not a single force or drive, but a complex composite. It has carried men to lofty heights of achievement and satisfaction. At the same time, it has plunged men to abysmal depths of bestiality and despair. Witness in the last half-century the constructive effort of Sir Winston Churchill as opposed to the destructive stigma of Adolf Hitler—in both cases, highly motivated men and dedicated to a cause. Medical science is now probing the motivational forces which cause self-realization and self-destruction. Failure has been shown, for example, to be mainly self-willed. That is to say, scientists are discovering what philosophers have said for ages: that talking success and thinking failure will reward one with the latter.

Motivation hits pretty close to home for the salesman. He is a student of "peaks and valleys." He knows when he is motivated he sells; when he isn't, he doesn't. He knows all too well that worse than this oscillation is a protracted plateau—a period of no growth and only pretended development. This is sometimes called a slump. At no time is the temptation to cheat greater than now. This is the supreme test. How the salesman handles his first slump frequently answers the question of whether he belongs or not. It all falls back to attitude. If he sees his slump as his manager's problem or the fault of a colleague or customer, or if he attempts to alibi his way out of it, *selling is not for him.* He would be doing himself, his associates, and his profession a real service if he got out—immediately and completely. A salesman who cannot make it with one company will not make it with another. Parenthetically speaking, the reason I can write this book for all salesmen, no matter what they are selling, is because selling is selling, the world over. There is only one way of getting off a plateau or out of a selling slump; and that is, getting off one's bottom. Work finds motivation only resting, waiting to be roused. And by work I refer only to directed effort with enlightened practice. To put it another way, using what you know as intelligently as your wits will allow. Work never means motion, per se. Ergo, a slump can be a good thing, reminding us that we are indeed coasting while our target drifts further from our sights.

Enlarging on our definition of motivation, let us state that it is the behavior instigated by *needs within* and directed towards *goals without* designed to satisfy these needs. This definition encompasses the broad framework of what has been called the *motivational cycle*. This cycle explains the mechanical steps or stages involved in motivation. Incidentally, it throws some light on why sophisticated modern man encounters so much difficulty sustaining his motivation (see Figure 1, page 150, Motivational Cycle). The cycle:

Stage 1   NEED. A lack of something or a deficit condition would explain this first stage. In general, the terms *needs, wants, desires,* or *motives* are to be used synonymously. Let us imagine that a man is hungry. An empty stomach would trigger this need.

Stage 2   UNCONSCIOUS TENSION BUILDUP. Either a conscious or an unconscious physical tension buildup may be caused by a need. In the case of hunger, there would be a sense of "feeling hungry"—of experiencing hunger pains.

Stage 3   FORCE. This is a drive or impetus which has been provided by a need, want, desire, or motive. You are hungry and in some discomfort. You must obtain food. This implies that you must act—you must do something *now*.

Stage 4   BEHAVIORAL ACTIVITIES, The actions, both mental and physical, brought into play in satisfying a need will be your next consideration. You go to the refrigerator for a midnight snack to satisfy your need for food.

Stage 5   GOAL. The object or incentive towards which behavioral activities are directed would be your goal. To quiet your growling stomach and be able to get some sleep, you raid the refrigerator.

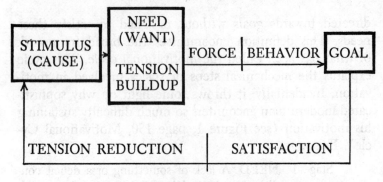

Figure 1: Motivational Cycle.

Stage 6   SATISFACTION. In eating this food, you have obtained your goal of hunger satisfaction. Your pain vanishes.

Stage 7   TENSION REDUCTION. A state of equilibrium has been obtained. When your need for food has been satisfied, you are no longer hungry. Your stomach stops growling. You can now sleep.

Remember, in human behavior there is always a motive or need and behind this, the cause. There is a push from inside the person to act in a certain way and not a pull from the outside. That is why self-management and self-discipline must emanate from within the salesman, not from without. In the case of the latter, this is a fabrication or a pose—a lie. It has no real value to the man in question. Doubtlessly, he will go through the motions to satisfy the pull from without. But unless he is convinced that it will meet a personal need within, it will not take hold of him. This is certain, no matter how great the outside pressure.

Recently a young manager who had once worked for me wrote about one of his "problem salesmen." This particular manager is a precise planner and dedicated to de-

150

tail. It so happens that I know the difficult salesman, too. He is not nearly as organized as his boss, nor need he be. He functions best when he has a lot of room to move in and a general outline to follow. To satisfy his manager he was, nevertheless, planning to copious lengths and turning these plans in faithfully. One day this manager and salesman were working together. It soon became apparent that the salesman was not using his planning at all. Shocked, the manager gave the salesman a crushing reprimand and even thought of firing him on the spot. My reply to my friend enjoined him to ask himself why the salesman did not use his planning, and then why planning was so important to him. Herein lies the answer to both problems, the manager's as well as the salesman's.

The example of food in the motivational cycle was an apt one because this is a physical need clearly discernible to everyone. This cycle is repeated again and again through each day of our lives. On the other hand, this closed circuit concept includes a major oversimplification—it tends to lump physical and psychological goals together. This is not wise. For many psychological, as distinct from physical, goals are not finite and specific. One can consume a specific quantity of food and thereby temporarily stop feeling hungry. It is doubtful that one can consume a specific quantity of prestige, for instance, and feel sated. Moreover, the need for an individual to feel superior, important, special, or dominant may never be satisfied sufficiently to inactivate the cause or causes. Craving or obsession, consequently, often replace simple need.

You have already been exposed to concepts which should create a desire to buy your product, service, or idea. Now, let us briefly consider what you require in order to activate your selling skills. Imagine yourself performing very well in the category of small business or marginal accounts, but unable to operate with an equal degree of success in the area of large potential. You may recognize yourself in this picture. If so, have you ever asked yourself why? Let us assume that a salesman has difficulty with large prospects. Could these be contributing factors to this behavior?

1. He fears entering the executive suite.
2. He is unable, or lacks belief in his ability to cope with questions, problems, or contingencies that might arise.
3. He enjoys personally dealing with people close to the job.
4. He has had a rather shattering experience in dealing with a large account.
5. Through an honest misunderstanding, he believes only his manager is meant to handle this business.
6. He is impatient with the planning and the protracted effort involved in large-account selling.

This, of course, doesn't even begin to cover all the foibles which may get in the way of a salesman doing his job. You can see, I'm sure, from this review, that many complex factors vie for your devotion to duty. They cannot be ignored.

How to Make Motivation Work for You

In the first chapter (see page 22) Selling and Confidence, you were introduced to a list of drive patterns which might possibly interfere with your effective selling. Let us return to them now. We have already established that the intensity of these drives varies between us, but that it remains relatively constant within each individual. We know that these drives or behavioral patterns make us utter the things we say and accomplish the things we do. For this reason, among others, they have always been of special interest, if not concern, to managers and supervisors. But seldom have individual salesmen been given an opportunity to evaluate these drives and determine if they are helping or hindering them. As you consider the definitions and indicators for each of these drives which are to follow, use the technique of overview. That is, think how they relate to your present selling activities, giving special attention to your problem areas.

ACCEPTANCE *is a desire to be clearly understood.*

Indicators: You rough out many drafts; invite questions; talk to the point; put it in writing; repeat instructions; summarize decisions; favor only advantageous facts; have the last word; make no quick decisions; talk redundantly.

Problems: You take too much time; fail to learn instructions; drive people away; overwork orders; irritate others; arrive at untenable conclusions; insist on sympathy.

SECURITY *is a desire to plan the future.*

Indicators: You budget spending; plan vacations; travel at bargain rates; avoid risky sports; have a long employment record; go to church regularly; buy clothes out of season; save paper, ribbon, string; use top-interest banks; make your own house and car repairs; have a good insurance plan.

Problems: You resist new ideas; avoid challenges; seldom suggest anything new; won't ask questions; fear changes; worry all the time; will not take a chance; are a "yes" man.

ATTENTION *is a need to have personal recognition.*

Indicators: You criticize top policies; wear casual office clothes; arrive late; take unnecessary risks; sign name with flourish; use color ink; stress success; buy fad furniture; have "inside" story; wear bow tie; butt into conversations; have 50 years experience at 30; submit reports on successful ideas; hide failures.

Problems: You create disturbances; seldom give your attention; distract others; cause accidents; avoid routine; steal credit; gossip frequently; stretch facts to suit your end.

FRIENDSHIP *is a need to have sympathetic companions.*

Indicators: You are free with confidence; counsel prone; list problems; hurt easily; trust people; spend time with but few; go through the motions of listening; like to do favors to obligate others; have hot and cold moods; are overly solicitous of others; are in need of a listener; apt to place people on a pedestal; are a member of an inner circle; offended by casualness; agreeable to anything; develop confidential discussions.

Problems: You mix poorly; waste time talking; won't work with just "anybody"; require constant attention; feed on sympathy; maintain a friend or foe relationship with everybody; condone cliques; incur favoritism or bias charges.

OWNERSHIP *is a desire to take care of things.*

Indicators: You drive a clean car; won't break book binding; file back copies; have all gadgets working; keep things locked up; have two or more wrist watches; have personal things in your office; have parent's books; turn out lights; shut car motor off; keep clothes well-pressed; read "use" directions; cover lawn furniture.

Problems: You don't return borrowed tools; are an overly careful worker; change machines reluctantly; permit excessive maintenance; requisition unnecessary extras; take too much time to finish; permit use of seconds only; make things "your own."

STATUS *is the need to attain rank.*

Indicators: You carry a heavy wallet; drop important names; display citations; tip extravagantly; are on all prestigious mailing lists; feature personalized shirts; use foreign phrases; are above details; use attaché case; know right books, magazines, newspapers, and television programs; operate via secretary; maintain "right" charge accounts; cover luggage with travel labels; favor prestige brands; wear lapel pin; drive new car.

Problems: You have no genuine desire for promotion; don't improve your worldly lot; may become a follower; are satisfied with mediocrity; spend beyond your means; are not receptive to orders; create and feed jealousies; lose friends by boasting.

ASSOCIATION *is a need to be with people.*

Indicators: You seldom remain at home; pick up hitchhikers; leave last; draw how-to-get-there sketches; have a busy telephone; build a rumpus room; are active in civic affairs, social groups; talk to strangers; look for luncheon dates; tell stories; introduce self to all concerned; keep many irons in the fire; own card tables; see all visitors; arrange parties.

Problems: You don't do best alone; need close watching; condone "associations"; won't "stay put"; distract others frequently; spend much time away from productive work; find causes jamming up; ask for and expect social benefits.

RESPONSIBILITY *is a desire to do something worthwhile.*

Indicators: You help out others; take over for the boss; volunteer for tough assignments; take the blame; are a company man; work as plant or office paper reporter; say and mean "the show must go on"; question method of income; aren't easily discouraged; are a problem solver; overcome weather obstacles; research to solve problems; work in the evenings; talk self-employment; are not interested in vacations.

Problems: You are a poor follower; want challenging work; chase new jobs; won't perform menial tasks; are dissatisfied with routine work; won't take a higher position; avoid important work; stay long on coffee breaks.

ACCOMPLISHMENT *is the need to work on a schedule.*

Indicators: You treat important and unimportant tasks alike; you beat the whistle; ask for work; bull your way through a schedule without deviation; keep promises; use check

156

sheets; say, "better do it myself" and do; work in any weather; talk pieces, hours, miles, time; are critical of delays; hate to do it over; are a self-starter; have a good filing system; tend to be haphazard in your solutions.

Problems: You flare up often; need needling; make unnecessary mistakes; are easily frustrated; challenge routine; create tools and equipment loss; break lines of communication often; want the same job.

RIGHTEOUSNESS *is the need to practice well-defined principles.*

Indicators: You avoid borrowing; are a company man; use your own car; submit accurate expense accounts; want to know the reason why; play poor office politics; tend to judge others; are often inconsiderate; turn in found articles; let it be known you are not a friendship buyer; can't act casually; row always against the stream; stick to your guns; make outside calls from toll booths; dislike compromise; go to church regularly; enjoy proving others wrong.

Problems: You don't follow blindly; won't compromise; are inflexible; make biased decisions; are frequently intolerant; vacillate often; are influenced by sympathy; have a weakness for preaching.

Don't expect any of these drive pattern identities to fit your psychic situation perfectly or to express your particular problem or concern exactly. They won't. This is only a guidance system. Use it as such to assist you in recognizing certain drives within you and others and then expand upon this understanding when you're selling. As you become more familiar with your drive patterns, then, it will become less difficult for you to identify with Mr. Prospect's.

How to Use Incentives

Yet another factor which complicates a salesman's behavior further is the area of incentives. Mistakenly, these are sometimes considered synonymous with motives or needs. They are not. As stated earlier in this discussion, motives are driving forces within the individual which dominate a desire to reach a goal or obtain a reward. At the same time, it is the incentive which makes the goal more attractive. For example, you may have a driving desire to become a manager or executive (this is your motive). Knowing that your company has an established policy of promoting from within (this is your incentive), spurs you on to extra effort and achievement.

Is it becoming clearer why you have chosen this profession over others? Can you now see selling as a career beyond simple economic expedience? Probably a great deal more of yourself has been given to this vocation than you realize. On the other hand, each of us sees light in a different fashion. This is how the selling profession was expressed by some of whom I queried:

    ** "I am a salesman because I like people; I like to be needed and to be useful."

    ** "Selling is the most fascinating thing I've ever done. Never have I been exposed to such challenging and interesting people as my customers."

    ** "I am doing much better than my father. He is proud of my success and I am happy because of this."

** "You cannot imagine doing anything else after you have once sold. The freedom and independence you have are really unbelievable."

** "In selling you set your own income and standard of living. I like that."

** "It is difficult for me to put into words the sense of satisfaction, power, and triumph one feels when the prospect signs that order!"

** "It's the first job I've ever had where I felt I belonged. You know what I mean, really belonged; I owe everything to selling."

** "This is the purest profession of them all. Everyone sells—the teacher, the preacher, the politician, the parent, the doctor—everybody. They all take their cue from us."

This list alone could fill a book. Write down all the reasons you like selling. Ask your colleagues to do the same. Then, compare lists. With practice you will be able to identify their drive pattern, not to mention your own.

And finally, so that you may be assisted further in determining what makes you go, let us consider some fundamentals of your personality. For our purposes, they are perception, thinking, and feeling.

Perception relates to the way we "see (that is, interpret) people and the things around them." What's more, it involves the meaning we attach to what we see, hear, taste, smell, or touch. What is so intriguing about perception is its highly subjective nature. That is, we see what we want to see. Our own personal blindness, in other words, prevents us from understanding the motivation of others. Though our eyes may be open, our heads and hearts remain closed to what is there. Alerted to this situation, one's mind can be trained to better perceive what is already perceptible to others.

Thinking, on the other hand, relates to a complex of retained experience and our perception of the present. Know that your thoughts are greatly influenced by your state of mind and feelings. It is precisely for this reason that you cannot think clearly when you are emotionally disturbed. Now, in this context, recall the definition of worry: a state of mind before a thing happens. Far better minds than mine have cautioned mankind of this fact. Yet, worry we will.

Feelings and emotions are the responses that influence our perception, learning, and in the end—our performance. What may trigger a favorable response in you may not move me a bit, or conversely, you. Can you see how reflecting on what rouses you to action, favorable or otherwise, may hold the key to your success as a salesman? As a man?

The fact that motivational studies have been prepared, usually for managers—to be used to train and motivate men—seems tantamount to putting the cart before the horse. Motivation is a force within, not without. Each of us has a unique complex of forces directing us towards our destiny. For a salesman to decipher this code would be many times more valuable than for his management to do it for him. Though understanding what we really want out of life and why we are accomplishing what we are doing is never easy to uncover, the search must nevertheless go on. Though we may aspire to what others have considered foolish or impractical, we must stand our ground in the knowledge that it is right for us. We must feed our drives the nourishment which will sustain us on our road to achievement. At the same time, we must curb our appetite for drives which are preventing us from becoming what we could become.

A paradox of life is that nearly all of us have little appreciation of our latent talent. This implies that our sight is generally far shorter than our reach. In selling we have the business of setting goals for ourselves periodically. Once set, these objectives so often get lost in the obfuscating rush of daily living. But if we could simply keep our attention upon these goals, despite the distractions, they would soon be ours. Something in front of us beckons us onward and upward. Goals, then, are one of the tools giving us directional pursuit. Such incentives as seeing in our future a new house, car, personal gift, education for a child, membership in a club, or a vacation to some favorite retreat spurs us on to these goals. Should you be concerned about becoming sated, take heart in knowing that fulfillment only stimulates new values and needs.

This exposure has given you some background on your motivational drives or reasons for succeeding. If you now believe dreams and aspirations can change from fantasies to concrete realities, you have gotten a piece of this montage. If you have also felt enthusiasm can be a driving force towards achievement, you have gotten another piece. If you recognize frustration and anxiety as normal companions, but no longer the controlling and demanding nemesis they heretofore have been, you have still another piece. And if you have discovered that all of us have a driving force to be complete, whatever that may entail, you have the total picture of what being a man as well as a salesman involves.

SELF-STUDY QUESTIONS:

1. Reference has been made to the "peaks and valleys" of selling. This is quite normal and to be expected. There are, however, a few who would remain blind to the lessons inherent in these career fluctuations. Low in motivation and with little pride in themselves or their profession, they operate much like Mr. Know-It-All.

Mr. Know-It-All has been a salesman for two years. He has had only indifferent success. Though long past his training period, his company continues to reimburse him beyond his productivity in the hopes of him soon finding himself in selling.

When asked by an acquaintance why he was selling, he replied sardonically, "It's a job. Beats working for a liv'n like you." Closer scrutiny of this young salesman reveals many things, not the least of which is the fact that he revels in talking.

"I don't have a thing in common with these guys. Not that they're not okay, ya know. Just, well, that they're not my speed. Whoever dug these people up threw the spade away and used a broom. That's for sure! Why, I could sell rings around this outfit without gett'n out of bed. Tell me this company isn't some kind of joke! Feature this, friend, we're trying to sell the same stuff Acme peddles. But get this —for twice the price. I tell you, it's unreal!" Before you have a chance to challenge his thinking, he continues, "They've got me carrying this terrific service load. Me! The best salesman in the territory. While they're gett'n rich doing noth'n, I'm gett'n headaches carrying them. Do they keep me busy? You bet they do! Afraid to give me breath'n room for fear I'll put them to shame. Hell, I could do this routine stand'n on my head. Say, tell your boss if he's look'n for a good salesman to give me a ring. Believe me, pal, I'm available!"

Consider Mr. Know-It-All only in the context of motivation. What do you think went wrong or awry with his motivation? What drive patterns can you identify? Would you attempt to help him? How? Have you ever met such a character? If you have, do you think he was aware of his problem? Assuming that he has the intelligence, aptitude, and potential to be a good salesman, how long would you give him before you would give up on him? Explain.

2. In this chapter, the author told you of his early career in selling and how it all happened. Reread this and consider these questions:

   a. What was his principal drive?
   b. Explain the motivational factors which influenced his development.
   c. Does this seem like an experience similar (dissimilar) to your own? Explain.
   d. What did the author do to accomplish his goals?
   e. What did you learn from this discussion or chapter to better understand his ultimate decision?

3. Write a 500-word essay on how motivation has related to your career to this moment.

RECOMMENDED FURTHER READING:

C. J. Adcock. *Fundamentals of Psychology* (Penguin Books, 1959).

U. S. Anderson. *The Magic in Your Mind* (Thomas Nelson & Sons, 1961).

Dalbir Bindra and Jane Stewart. *Motivation* (Penguin Modern Psychology, 1966).

J. A. C. Brown. *The Social Psychology of Industry* (Penguin Books, 1954) and *Techniques of Persuasion* (Penguin Books, 1963).

Wm. S. Casselberry, Ph.D. *How to Work Miracles in Your Life* (Parker Publishing Company, Inc., 1964).

Gilbert P. Edwards. *Psycho-Recording: The Secrets of Mental Vision* (Prentice-Hall, Inc., 1967).

Charles D. Flory. *Managers for Tomorrow* (A Mentor Book, 1967).

Vernon Howard. *The Magic Power of Command Transmission* (Prentice-Hall, Inc., 1965).

Elbert Hubbard. *The Philosophy of Elbert Hubbard* (Wm. H. Wise & Company, 1930).

Ignace Lepp. *The Psychology of Loving* (A Mentor-Omega Book, 1963).

Ken Kesey. *Sometimes a Great Notion* (The Viking Press, 1964).

Harold J. Leavitt. *Managerial Psychology* (The University of Chicago Press, 1958).

Bernard Malamud. *The Fixer* (Farrar, Straus, and Giroux, 1966).

Edward J. Murray. *Motivation and Emotion* (Prentice-Hall, Inc., 1964).

Vance Packard. *The Pyramid Climbers* (McGraw-Hill Book Company, Inc., 1962).

Jean Rostand. *Human Heredity* (Philosophical Library, Inc., 1961).

Baruch Spinoza. *How to Improve Your Mind* (The Citadel Press, 1962).

Richard C. Teevan and Robert C. Birney. *Theories of Motivation in Learning* (D. Van Nostrand Company, Inc., 1964).

James K. Van Fleet. *How to Use the Dynamics of Motivation* (Parker Publishing Company, Inc., 1967).

Gaston Viaud. *Intelligence: Its Evolution and Forms* (Harper & Brothers, 1960).

The Wall Street Journal. "The New Millionaires and How They Made Their Fortunes" (Bernard Geis Associates, 1960).

(6) The Finishing Touch for Confident Selling

"The most important thing you've got to do is decide what you want to do. Once you've made that decision, the rest is easy."

These words were addressed to me by a friend. He is the owner and operator of a small publishing company. A few years ago he decided what he wanted. Since that time he has been making rapid progress in the direction of that goal. Publisher of a customized pricing service for the plumbing, heating, and air-conditioning industry, he has allowed nothing to distract him from this singular objective. What's more, his vocation and avocation have combined to give him a united thrust. You could never meet a more dedicated or enthusiastic person in work. This man literally lives to work. One of the curious things about him, though, is that he is a terrific salesman, but doesn't consider himself one. To appreciate what an effective salesman

166

he is, consider a recent selling trip he took to Indiana, Illinois, and Kansas. He told me of his plans and what he expected to accomplish. Listening to him detail his planning with such enthusiasm was music to this sales manager's ears, even if it did tax his sense of credulity. One could not help but be impressed by the confidence in his voice and the glint in his eye. He had worked hard to develop a good product—a product that is needed in his industry. At the same time, he had obviously made every effort to understand and anticipate the problems confronting his customers and prospects alike. He displayed confidence in the knowledge that he had the answers. As I studied him, I was mentally reassured that no prospect would unsell him on this point. Ten days later, he returned with enough business to require the addition of another permanent member to his staff. Incidentally, he accomplished exactly what he had planned to do.

As much as I was impressed with this effort, I realized that he had no doubt that he would be successful. Then too, I knew that every moment he was on that trip he was selling or thinking of selling. His whole being, in other words, was concentrated on bringing home the business. So busy was he apparently that there was no time for fear, or worry, or interference of any kind, preventing him from doing his appointed task. Absolutely everything was working for him. It was impossible for him to fail. He only thought and expected one thing, success, and he was awarded the same.

On the other hand, had he failed, he would have taken small comfort in the inventions of failure. That is, the excuses we are prone to invent for not succeeding. Moreover, if he had brought home an impressive assortment of "gonna buys," he would have realized better than anyone that he had next to nothing. An employer knows only too well that you can't eat promises.

Imagine what it would be like if all salesmen could be imbued with the spirit of my friend; if they could see themselves as running their own businesses; if they could decide what they wanted to do and then, do it; if they could think and expect success, finding no solace in near success, whatever that may be; if they could have that same contagious confidence that puts people at ease; and finally, if they could forget themselves in work, worrying little how they might appear to others.

Conquering Fear of Failure

A more typical attitude, I'm afraid, is illustrated by this true incident. Sales meetings, as you may know, require careful planning, skillful execution, and near flawless closing. Otherwise, they miss their mark completely. When I was in industry, we had a policy in my firm of holding quarterly seminars composed of four districts. It fell to one district manager to be the host, once per year. Each manager, of course, tried to outdo his peers. After one such meeting, which had been of particular success, everyone was congratulating the host. He took this praise well enough, but then turned the focus back on his would-be adulators with this question, "Why do you think I worked so hard on this meeting, anyway?" Surprised by this remark, there followed a dead silence matched only by many puzzled expressions. He continued, "I'll tell you why. It was simply a matter of fear—fear of failure, period." This candid admission cracked open the silence to some frank exchanges. They all followed the fear line and were summed up in this comment, "I guess you could say that the shoe fits me as well. No one likes to get hammered." Finally, as if an afterthought, I was asked my view. I had the great temptation to concur with the others—to fit snugly into their fear syndrome. But I had thought too much about this subject and had worked too hard to conquer fear to con myself now. "I suppose what drives me to do my best more than anything else," I said seriously, "is the effective utilization of my inherent ability." The reaction quite predictably was immediate. It was echoed around the room with this needling phrase, "How did we ever get a guy like you in this outfit?" Once the laughter had subsided, I smiled and offered my own brand of levity, "Isn't it just a matter of chemistry, gentlemen—opposite charges attracting?" Yet, even in this jesting, there was a grain of truth. What I was actually expressing was the positive counterpart of the negative fear.

Man has always had a strange fascination for fear. In preparing my notes for this final chapter, I consulted *The Oxford Dictionary of Quotations* where this fact was brought home to me with some force. While I could find only five references to confidence, more than 150 separate entries were indexed for fear. Courage had 30 listings. Somewhat disappointed, nonetheless, with these expressions, I turned to the writings of Ralph Waldo Emerson to see how he viewed fear and courage:

ON FEAR: He has not learned the lesson of life who does not every day surmount a fear . . . Fear always springs from ignorance . . . Men suffer all their life long under the foolish superstition that they can be cheated. But it is as impossible for a man to be cheated by anyone but himself, as for a

169

thing to be and not to be at the same time.

ON COURAGE: What a new face courage puts on everything! A determined man, by his very attitude and the tone of his voice, puts a stop to defeat and begins to conquer.

Many books, articles, and seminars emphasize the "peak" aspect of selling or the promised cornucopia of sales attainment. They ride a wave of emotion and tie their message to enthusiasm. The euphoric value of such exposure cannot be denied; nor can the fact that these techniques are of only ephemeral influence or value. Cursory methods, of course, fail to probe and unlock the pent-up self-doubts, fears, and false images many salesmen continue to harbor—emotional obstacles which may prevent them from doing their best. Permit me to explain.

Salesmen are uncomfortable. Being treated in many cases like punch cards spewing from EDP systems, they have found themselves confronting an awesome but manageable technology. And in addition, they have another confrontation to consider, themselves. On the one hand, they are holding their own; on the other, they don't appear so sure-footed. The mounting pressure of this polarity may be likened to the following dilemma:

Imagine there is a wall. In this wall are two doorways. One has a bulletproof translucent glass; the other, nothing but air. Both appear to the naked eye equally accessible. There is a 50–50 chance that the person attempting to walk through these archways will be shockingly and abruptly halted by a barrier. Then again, he may enter with ease. Psychologically, if he is confronted by many translucent but solid obstacles, he will become quite hesitant, if not apprehensive. Possibly, he will begin to conclude that all doorways are barriers. When he sees such a pattern as this, consequently, he pretends to himself that it is indeed not approachable; and so he continues on his way, leaving it and those like it unchallenged. Eventually, he finds himself limited to precious few portals.

A clear-cut advantage of one product over another is rapidly vanishing. Competition is extremely keen. This is an ideal situation for true salesmanship. Moreover, the old idea that you must believe in your company, product, service, and self was never more valid. But that is precisely the point. It is becoming more and more difficult for the salesman to find the will to believe, to know whom to trust, and to be satisfied that he is not being duped. A complex individual, as he becomes more aware of self, he feels the scathing heat of competition. Add to this the general complexity of life itself, with all its energy-sapping and conflicting demands on his person, and you have a measure of the dimensions of his dilemma.

Salesmen are suffering. At this moment they are suffering from unlimited opportunity being stifled by a single insurmountable barrier—self. More sophisticated, better educated, and in possession of the most elaborate network of technological aids, they are always on the brink of great things, but never seem to quite turn that final corner to success. They cannot master or effectively negotiate that one remaining obstacle—self. All the imaginable theories and tools are implemented to put them on a track to the effective utilization of their ability; all, that is, but the one which would put them into the center of their problem—self.

In a whirlwind effort to master the forces and challenges facing the salesman today, all available skill has been focused on creating an environment conducive to productive work. But the light always emanates from outside the man. He remains vulnerable, as do we all, to the forces which emanate from within. These are our drives or emotional need responses. Controlled and channeled, they make for smooth sailing. Unchecked or unnoticed, they consume a man and reduce him to the pulp of the man he was or could become.

Salesmen Are Individuals

In a word, not enough has been or is being done to harness the potential locked in the salesman as an individual. Goethe saw this promise,

> If you treat an individual as he is, he will stay as he is. But if you treat him as if he were what he ought to be and could be, he will become what he ought to be and could be.

Needless to say, a salesman has much less reason today not to become what he could become. Sociology and social and educational psychology are behavioral sciences which could help him get on the track with great speed. But these social sciences, not to mention the humanities and philosophical studies, seldom find their way into the fabric of sales training programs. All available time is taken up with how to sell and what to sell, with a dash of the "rah-rah" gender of inspirational guidance. This has already proven inadequate, if not anachronistic. A salesman today must know why to sell as well.

Consider this a moment. His curiosity is stimulated very early in life. It is cultivated and fed intellectually in school. And, then, once school days are over, it is coldly applied to things as he takes up his profession. Why does a certain machine give so much horsepower? How much heat is generated from an exothermic chemical reaction? Things—things—always things outside the man. But the why that bombards the salesman's mind every day of his life does not always relate to things. Regrettably, this turns to frustration as he tries to interpret and apply his tools of things to abstract questions of why. He tries to solve his problem with the "tools of how" before the problem is clearly defined in his mind. The fact that the problem is people and not machines or mathematics, throws him into a quandary. For this very reason, he is apt to deny its existence—which only makes matters worse.

No different than people in general, the salesman wants to be appreciated as a whole man. This means that he is not satisfied with money alone as an incentive. He wants a sense of accomplishment as well as a feeling of value. Compensation, then, must include a generous supply of recognition, acceptance, prestige, status, and achievement, in addition to security. It is such psychic replenishment that sustains the salesman's momentum. And conversely, the absence of which, produces his inertia.

Selling is most demanding of intelligence, drive, determination, and tenacity—resources which are quite dependent upon emotional stability. Though products and services have become streamlined and refined for greater efficacy, salesmen have changed their approach to the problem of selling very little. Mass advertising, complex distributing techniques, sociomarketing schemes, and elaborate sales aids notwithstanding, person-to-person confrontations remain pitifully inadequate—obsolescent strategies. So obsessed with the business of things, too often salesmen have been created, produced, packaged, and distributed like the impersonal wares that they would sell. Small wonder that this is not working. A quiet rebellion is underway as the per capita productivity of individual salesmen continues to drop. As this very reactionary generation takes over, this may well become open rebellion. In a word, the salesman is tired of being treated like an impersonal commodity.

But before such an explosion occurs, something can be done. For one thing, the job can be made to match the needs of the man instead of the man matching the needs of the job. This requires each salesman to be treated exactly as an individual. His potential can be explored by listening to him, studying his observations and comments, and by accepting him as an integral part of the marketing team. Were this to be done and no more, each man's value to his employer, not to mention himself, would increase tenfold.

Khalil Gibran once wrote, "Work is love made visible." There is much love to be found in selling. A salesman can take this abstraction and translate it into the satisfaction he feels when he has done a good job and a customer says, "Thank God, we've got you to depend on," or when he answers an urgent call with the badly needed information a customer requires. Wilfred A. Petersen claimed "Success is 99% mental attitude. It calls for love, joy, optimism, confidence, serenity, poise, faith, courage, cheerfulness, imagination, initiative, tolerance, honesty, humility, patience, and enthusiasm." John Lennon of the Beatles said it well but only in a more contemporary idiom:

> Everyone can be a success; if you keep saying that enough times to yourself you can be. We're no better than anybody else. We're all the same. We're as good as Beethoven. Everyone's the same inside. You need the desire and the right circum-

stances, but it's nothing to do with talent or with training or education. You get primitive painters and writers don't you? Nobody told them how to do it. They told themselves they could do it and just did it . . .

Overcoming Fear with Confidence

Another way this might be said is that if a salesman can see himself doing a job, making a sale, or getting a promotion, he will no doubt realize it. Provided, of course, that he tells himself he will do it and then actually takes action.

Next to fear, the most elusive mental image is confidence. Confidence is purely and simply a state of mind. You can't buy it, bargain for it, or in any way realize it outside yourself. It must come from within. And those that would flaunt it with reckless abandon usually possess little, if any, of this precious "mind dust." Another human tendency seems to be the reading of confidence and strength into others while registering inferiority and doubt in ourselves. That is to say, we have a tendency to make "other people" possessors of Godlike qualities. To compensate there is the temptation to assert ourselves too strenuously, promise beyond our capacity to deliver, and exaggerate to the point of absurdity. Genuine confidence is essential to a salesman for these expressed reasons.

Take heart in knowing that every man on earth, no matter how noble or exalted, wears a mask. Beyond this facade a spirit moves, harboring the same feelings as you. Know yourself and you will know and understand him. And in this knowledge you will find confidence. A salesman so endowed will be a free man—free of worry and frustration.

This is what I have learned and what I now impart to you. It has been my guiding light. Don't be dismayed if you have learned nothing new. Take comfort in these words of Elbert Hubbard:

> So then if I tell you a thing you already know, I confer on you the great blessing of introducing you to yourself and of giving you the consciousness that you know. And to know you know is power. And to feel the sense of power is to feel a sense of oneness with the Source of Power.

THE BEGINNING

SELF-STUDY QUESTIONS:

1. What—in your mind—represents the complete salesman? The complete man?

2. How would you compare your selling skills with the selling skills of the subject in the beginning of this chapter? How would you compare your colleagues' to his?

3. Dagobert D. Runes wrote of fear:

> Fear means nursing a problem instead of facing it. It is a play of self-pity, ignoring the inevitable. It takes courage to brush aside broodings of temerity. Our sages said that the courageous die by the blade, the timid by a thousand strokes of their fears.

   Do you subscribe to this philosophy? Explain?

4. Define in your own terms what these words mean to you in the light of your own experience:
   - Enthusiasm
   - Confidence
   - Worry
   - Fear
   - Doubt
   - Success
   - Failure
   - Happiness
   - Love
   - Frustration
   - Anxiety

5. If you could have a person-to-person chat with the author, what would you wish to ask him?

177

RECOMMENDED FURTHER READING:

Robert Ardrey. *The Territorial Imperative* (Atheneum, 1966).

Sholem Asch. *One Destiny* (G. P. Putnam's Sons, 1945).

Irwin Edman. *Philosopher's Holiday* (The Viking Press, 1938).

Jay E. Greene, Ph.D. *100 Great Thinkers* (Washington Square Press, Inc., 1967).

Cameron Hawley. *The Lincoln Lords* (Little, Brown, and Company, 1960).

Eric Hoffer. *The Passionate State of Mind* (Harper & Row, 1954) and *The Ordeal of Change* (Harper & Row, 1952).

David Hume. *An Enquiry Concerning Human Understanding* (Washington Square Press, Inc., 1963).

Arnold A. Hutschnecker, M.D. *The Will to Live* (Thomas Y. Crowell, 1951).

Aldous Huxley. *Point Counter-Point* (Penguin Books, 1955).

John F. Kennedy. *Profiles in Courage* (Harper & Row, 1955).

Meyer Levin. *Compulsion* (Simon and Schuster, 1956).

David J. Schwartz, Ph.D. *The Magic of Psychic Power* (Parker Publishing Company, Inc., 1966).

Florence Scovel Shinn. *The Game of Life and How to Play It* (Gerald J. Rickard, 1941).

Thomas Sugrue. *There Is a River* (Henry Holt & Co., Inc., 1942).

Alfred North Whitehead. *The Aims of Education* (The New American Library, 1949).

INDEX

A

Absenteeism, 24
Acceptance, 153
Accomplishment, 156–157
Activities, behavioral, 149
Actors, film, 68
Alibi-itis, 37
Arguing, 78
Argumentative customer, 133–135
Aspirations, 108, 161
Association, 155–156
Assumptions, false or unwarranted, 94–97
Attention:
    absolute and undivided, 77
    drive, 154
Attitude:
    about selling as profession, 32–34
    account in constant trouble, 32
    affects salesman, 41–45
    anxiety and concern, 31
    believe in company, 57–58

Attitude (cont'd.)
    believe in yourself, 57
    can't seem to close, 31
    commandments of selling, 57–60
    constantly off-balance, 31
    controlled and enlightened, 55–57
    controlling, 49–55
    create something for others, 59
    driven or driving, 62
    enthusiasm, 60
    expect to sell, 58
    fighting worry, 45–48
    imagination, 61
    in command, 32–33
        create and meet needs, 32
        economic machinery of nation, 32
        employment opportunity, 32
        nation's development, 32
        powerful influence, 32
        prosperity, 32

Attitude (cont'd.)
    "salesman" who wins, 32
    scale of living, 33
    social well-being, 32
    when one sells something, 32
  introspection, 61
  logic, 61
  mind and destiny, 61–62
  mind load with tools, 61
  needed, salesmen are, 33
    benefits clients, 33
    help economy, 33
    moves the public, 33
  opportunity, you are, 33–34
    customers buy you, 34
    for others and self, 33–34
    others are changed, 34
  other-people oriented, 58–59
  plan work, work plan, 60
  preparation for sales call, 40
  problems as door openers, 59–60
  reason, 61
  see self as successful, 58
  selling not unlike hitting, 38–41
  slave rather than master, 32
  understanding yourself, 34–38
    (see also Self-understanding)
  vision, 61
  worry, a state of mind, 32

B

Behavioral activities, 149
Behavioral patterns, 68
Benefits, discussing, 83
Berne, 68
Books on selling, 39
Bryan, 62

C

Calls:
  decrease in number, 24
  preparation, 40

Change, prospect's reluctance to, 36, 90–91
Character, 107–108
Command, salesman in, 32–33
Comments, irrelevant, 80
Communication, 75–81 (see also Empathetic understanding)
Compensation, 173
Comprehension, speed, 116
Confidence and selling:
  answers to customers' problems, 167
  courage, 169
  drive patterns, list, 22
  emotionally taxing prospects, 23–24, 25–26
  every man wears mask, 175
  example, 166–167
  excessive emotional commitment, 22–23
  expecting success, 167
  fear, 168–171, 175–176
    failure, 168–171
    overcoming, 175–176
  good product, 167
  good salesman, 24–26
    fine sensitivity, 24
    healthy ego, 24
    high energy level, 24
    three essential parts, 24
  making others Godlike, 175
  possible interfering forces, 22
  sales as criteria, 26
  sales calls as criteria, 26
  salesmen as individuals, 172–175
    appreciated as whole man, 173
    compensation, 173
    exploring potential, 174
    feeling of value, 173
    inertia, 173
    matching job to man, 174
    sense of accomplishment, 173
  slowdown of salesman, 23–24, 25

Confidence and selling (cont'd.)
  absenteeism, 24
  contagious, 24
  drop in sales production, 24
  sales calls go down, 24
  selling impasse, 25
  worry, 24–25
  state of mind, 175
  veteran salesman, 23
Cooperation, encourage, 103–105
Courage, 169
Craving, 151
Creative ideas, kinetic energy, 143
Criteria of salesman, 26
Customers, tough, 124–135 (see also Persuasion)

D

Decorum, 70
Destructiveness, 78
Directed questions, 117
Distraction, 76
Dreams, 161
Drive patterns:
  acceptance, 153
  accomplishment, 156–157
  association, 155–156
  attention, 154
  friendship, 154
  intensity of drive, 152
  interfere with selling, 152
  list, 22
  ownership, 154–155
  responsibility, 156
  righteousness, 157
  security, 153
  status, 155

E

Economy, debilitated, 33
Ego, healthy, 24

Emerson, Ralph Waldo, 169
Emotional needs, exploiting:
  ask for comments, 83
  dictating what one buys, 83
  discussion of benefits, 83
  objections give clues, 84
  think, 84
  topics which evoke emotions, 83
Emotional recognition, 68
Emotional screen, 76
Emotions:
  excessive commitment, 22–23
  feelings and, 160
  mentality with, 146
  motivation, 146
  prospect's, 106–121 (see also Persuasion)
  sales call, 36
  vibrations, 40
Empathetic understanding:
  atmosphere of empathy, 68
  categorizing people, 65–66
  changing nuances, 66
  communication, 75–81
    hearing level, 75–76
    listening level, 75–79 (see also Listening)
    thinking level, 75, 79–81
  different types people, cultivate, 68
  emotional needs, exploiting, 83–84 (see also Emotional needs, exploiting)
  emotional needs of prospects, 69
  emotional recognition, 68
  film actor or scientist, 68
  Games People Play, 68–69
  ideas and behavioral patterns, 68
  individuals, not stereotypes, 66
  interpersonal forces, 68
  intuition, 66
  keys, 66–69
    craving approval, 67

Empathetic understanding (cont'd.)
  love ourselves, 67
    more interested in ourselves, 67
    need to feel important, 67
  mood and disposition, 66
  people as "menacing," 67
  prospect as person, 69–75
    create mirror image, 72
    disparities observed, 75
    how he sees you, 70
    how he thinks, 71
    how he thinks you see him, 70
    misinterpreting remarks, 71
    office, 72–74 (see also Office)
    self-image, 69, 72
    surroundings, 72–74
  rapport, 68
  salesman image, 70–71
    change, 71
    grooming and decorum, 70
    moderation, 70
    negative sales factors, 70
    never become personal, 71
  "stroke," 68
  study and evaluate prospect, 66
  taking worry out of selling, 68
  thinking about prospect, 79–82
    concrete replies, 79–80
    distaff side of his office, 82
    how he takes interruptions, 81, 82
    irrelevant comments, 80
    kind of person, 81–82
    listening technique, 81
    objections, 80
    office, open and available, 82
    peers, 82
    phone calls, 82
    superiors, 82
    supervisors, 82
    tone of voice, 81
    visualizing with words, 80
    what he doesn't say, 80–81

Empathetic understanding (cont'd.)
    words he uses, 80
  uncontrolled inherent nature, 68
Employment opportunity, 32
Energy level, high, 24
Enthusiasm, 161
Exhaustion, mental, 37
Explicit meaning, 76
Exploratory questions, 118

F

Failure:
  fear of, 168–179
  no excuses, 167
  no solace in near success, 168
  self-willed, 147–148
Fear:
  failure, 168–171
  overcoming with confidence, 175–176
Feelings and emotions, 160
Film actors, 68
Fitzgerald, F. Scott, 147
Force, 149
Friendship, 154
Fulfillment, 161

G

Games People Play, 68–69
Gibran, Khalil, 174
Glad-hander, 126–128
Goal, 149, 161
Goals without, 149
Goethe, 61
Grooming, 70
Guilt, 78

H

Habits, bad, 37
Hearing, three levels, 116
Hubbard, Elbert, 176

Human needs, 32
Human tendencies, 90–96
Hypothetical questions, 118

I

Identity, collective, 141
Imagination, a tool, 61
Implicit meaning, 76
Incentives, use, 158–161
Inertia, 173
Interests, 108
Interruptions, 81, 82
Intuition, 66
Irrelevancies, avoiding, 115

J

Justifying questions, 118

K

Knowledge, a tool, 36

L

Leading questions, 119
Lear, Bill, 146
Lennon, John, 174
Listening:
    checklist, 77–78
        absolute, undivided attention,
            77
        arguing, 78
        destructive talk, 78
        guilt, 78
        imposing your will, 77–78
        monopolizing presentation, 78
        use entire body, 77
    distraction, 76
    emotional screen, 76
    explicit and implicit meanings,
        76
    impediments, 76
    level of communication, 75

Listening (cont'd.)
    motivation, 76
    rebuttal instinct, 76
    wandering mind, 76
Literal meaning, 76
"Literature peddlers," 35
Living, scale, 33
Logic, a tool, 61
*Lost Generation Period of Amer-
    ican Literature,* 147

M

Managers, sales, 39
Meanings of words, 76
Mental exhaustion, 37
Methodical customer, 128–129
Moderation, salesman shows, 70
Money as motivator, 142, 143, 147
Motivation:
    always in human behavior, 150
    answers "inside you," 141
    attitude, 148 (*see also* Attitude)
    choice of profession, 158–159
    closed circuit concept, 151
    collective identity, salesmen, 141
    complex subject, 144
    craving or obsession, 151
    cycle, 149–150 (*see also* Mo-
        tivational cycle)
    defined, 144–147
    difficulty sustaining, 149
    dreams and aspirations, 161
    drive patterns, 152–158 (*see also*
        Drive patterns)
    enthusiasm, 161
    failure, self-willed, 147–148
    feelings and emotions, 160
    food, 151
    frustration, anxiety, depression,
        141, 161
    getting on with life, 140
    goals give directional pursuit, 161

Motivation (cont'd.)
  goals without, 149
  how to understand, 147–152
  incentives, 158–161
  individual uniqueness, 145
  individuals, salesmen, 141
  involves behavior, 144–145
  kinetic energy of creative ideas, 143
  lack, 76
  listening to inner calling, 145
  make it work, 152–158
  man and salesman, 161
  mentality and emotion, 146
  money, 142, 143, 147
    cover for deeper desire, 147
    idea of accumulating, 143
    insufficient compensation, 142
  more important than innate ability, 145
  needs within, 148
  not necessarily good, 147
  not single force or drive, 147
  "peaks and valleys," 148
  perception, 159
  physical and psychological goals, 151
  "problem salesman," 150–151
  protracted plateau, 148
  push from inside, 150
  reasons for succeeding, 146
  scoffers become sycophants, 146
  seeking what we don't want, 146–147
  self-management and self-discipline, 150
  selling is melting pot, 141
  setting goals periodically, 161
  slump, 148
  studies, 160
  teacher-pupil relationship, 143
  thinking, 160
  to be of value, 142

Motivation (cont'd.)
  total failure seldom occurs, 142
  under the microscope, 144
  what we want, 147
  why we seek what we want, 147
  without direction, 142
  work, definition, 148
Motivational cycle:
  behavioral activities, 149
  force, 149
  goal, 149
  need, 149
  satisfaction, 150
  steps or stages, 149
  tension reduction, 150
  unconscious tension buildup, 149
Motivational factors, 107–109
Motivational studies, 160

N

Nation's development, 32
Need:
  salesman, for, 33
  stage in *motivational cycle*, 149
Needs within, 148

O

Objections:
  evaluating, 123
  prospect's, 80–84
Objectives:
  eliminate worry and frustration, 27
  steps to accomplish, 28
  understanding between salesman and management, 27
Obsession, 151
Office:
  activity, 74
  appearance, 74
  books, magazines, newspapers, 72
  calendar, desk, 73

Office (cont'd.)
carpeted, 73
colors, 73
desk, 73
external order, 73
furnishings, 74
location, 72, 74
modus operandi, 73
open and available, 82
pictures, 72
reflects inner man, 72
relevant impressions, 74
show or work, 73
things displayed, 72
Open questions, 117
Opinionated customer, 130–132
Opportunity, salesman is, 33–34
Overcautious customer, 129–130
Ownership, 154–155
Oxford Dictionary of Quotations,
169

P

Perception, 159
Persuasion:
cooperation, encourage, 103–105
make prospect comfortable,
104–105
prospect's mood, observe, 104
purpose of call, state, 104
dealing with prospect's emotions,
109–121
accept his emotions uncriti-
cally, 110–111
activate his thinking, 116–119
awareness of his own feelings,
110
encourage expression, 109
feedback of thinking, 114
hold his attention, 114–116
listen to prospect, 111–114
proper resistance, 119–120
emotions of prospect, 106–121

Persuasion (cont'd.)
gaining skill, techniques, 103–
121
hearing, three levels, 116
human tendencies, 90–96
false or unwarranted assumptions, 94–96
prefer hearing what we want,
92–94
prefer own thoughts, 91–92
resistance to change, 90–91
long-term Master Plan, 99–103
motivational factors, 107–109
aspirations, 108
character or value system,
107–108
interests, 108
security, 108–109
status-striving drive, 108
offsetting invalid assumptions, 96–
97
planning, how it assists, 115–116
avoiding irrelevancies, 115
fresh information, 116
speeches kept short, 115–116
speed of comprehension, 116
sticking to point, 115
using repetition, 116
problem, sources, 89
questions, 117–119 (*see also*
Questions)
resistance, meeting effectively,
121–124
believe in him, 124
evaluating objections, 123
objection hopping, 123
prospect aware of resistance,
123
rationalizing, 122–123
trust him, 124
understanding, 123
unresponsive attitude, 122
vehemence, 122

Persuasion (cont'd.)
  thoughts of prospect, draw out,
    105–106
    prefacing key words, 106
    questions, 105–106
    repeat negative key words, 106
    summarize back, 106
  tough customers, 124–135
    argumentative, 133–135
    glad-hander, 126–128
    methodical, 128–129
    opinionated, 130–132
    overcautious, 129–130
    procrastinator, 126
    silent, 125
    skeptical, 132–133
  what you say, 115
Petersen, Wilfred A., 174
Planning:
  "problem salesmen," 150–151
  what it does, 115–116
Plateau, 148
Positive climate, 40
Procrastinator, 126
Production, sales, 24
Prospect, 65–84 (see also Empathetic understanding)
Prosperity, 32

Q

Questions:
  directed, 117
  exploratory, 118
  hypothetical, 118
  justifying, 118
  leading, 119
  open, 117
  reflective, 117
  restatement, 117–118
  summarizing, 118

R

Rapport, 68

Rationalizing, 122–123
Reason, a tool, 61
Rebuttal instinct, 76
Reflective questions, 117
Repetition, using, 116
Replies, concrete, 80
Resistance, meeting effectively, 121–124
Responsibility, 156
Restatement questions, 117–118
Righteousness, 157

S

Sales managers, 39
Salesman, what he is, 32–34 (see also Attitude)
Satisfaction, 150
Scale of living, 33
Scientists, 68
Security:
  common motivational factor, 108–109
  drive, 153
Self-discipline ,150
Self-image, 69, 72
Self-management, 150
Self-study questions, 85
Self-understanding:
  alibi-itis, 37
  bad habits, 37
  combatant prospect, 35
  educator and problem solver, 36
  emotional vibrations, 40
  emotions in sales call, 36
  full circle of experience, 37
  image you project, 37
  knowledge, a tool, 36
  "literature peddlers," 35
  mental exhaustion, 37
  platitudes and jargon, 36
  positive climate, 40
  preparing for call, 40

Self-understanding (cont'd.)
  press or impress, 37
  prospect's reluctance to change,
    36
  reading selling books, 39
  review know-how, 38
  sales managers, 39
  sales training, 35
  self-imposed pressure, 37
  self-pity, self-indulgence, 37
  "selling streaks," 39
  sensitivity or awareness, 34
  study art of selling, 39
  study successes, 38, 39
  thinking negatively, 41
  veteran salesmen, 37
  worrying, not working, 37
Selling (*see also* specific items)
  attitude, 31–64
  confidence, 21–30
  difficulty with large prospects,
    152
  finishing touch, 166–178
  fortuitous vocation, 142
  melting pot, 141
  motivation, 140–165
  obsolescent strategies, 173
  "peak" aspect, 170
  persuasion, 87–139
  understanding, 34–38, 65–86
    (*see also* Understanding)
"Selling streaks," 39
Sensitivity of good salesman, 24
Silent customer, 125
Skeptical customer, 132–133
Slowdown of salesman, 23–24, 25
  (*see also* Confidence and sell-
    ing)
Slump, 148
Speeches, 115–116
Status, 155
Status-striving drive, 108
Stereotypes, 66

"Stroke," 68
Success, reasons for, 146
Surroundings of prospect, 72–74

T

Talents, latent, 161
Tension:
  unconscious buildup, 149
  reduction, 150
Thinking:
  level of communication, 75, 79–
    81
  motivation, 160
Thoreau, Henry David, 145
Thoughts, prospect's, 105–106 (*see
  also* Persuasion)
Tone of voice, 81
Training, sales, 35
Trust, 124

U

Understanding:
  between salesman and manage-
    ment, 27
  difficult people, 123
  empathetic, 65–86 (*see also* Em-
    pathetic understanding)
  express, 123
  yourself, 34–38 (*see also* Self-
    understanding)
Unresponsiveness, 122

V

Value system, 107–108
Vehemence, 122
Vision, a tool, 61
Voice, tone, 81

W

Words:
  kind used by prospect, 80
  meanings, 76
Work, defined, 148
Worry, 24–25, 27, 32, 45–48